Creating the
Accountability Culture

Creating the Accountability Culture

The Science of Life Changing Leadership

Yvonne Thompson

BUSINESS EXPERT PRESS

Creating the Accountability Culture: The Science of Life Changing Leadership

Copyright © Business Expert Press, LLC, 2018.

First published in 2018 by
Business Expert Press, LLC
222 East 46th Street, New York, NY 10017
www.businessexpertpress.com

ISBN-13: 978-1-94819-878-3 (paperback)
ISBN-13: 978-1-94819-879-0 (e-book)

Business Expert Press Human Resource Management and Organizational Behavior Collection

Collection ISSN: 1946-5637 (print)
Collection ISSN: 1946-5645 (electronic)

Cover and interior design by Exeter Premedia Services Private Ltd., Chennai, India

First edition: 2018

10 9 8 7 6 5 4 3 2 1

Printed in the United States of America.

Abstract

Our world seems to be changing and evolving more rapidly than any other time in history. Change is being felt in all sectors and all areas of business, from our world economy and environmental considerations, to the younger employees seeking new ways to contribute and demanding new work environments. The many factors we are facing require that we take a serious look at our business and human resource practices.

This work takes a close look at the challenges we are all facing and proposes an entirely new way of building corporate culture. Tools and techniques for shifting our present culture of victimization and disempowerment to full accountability and responsibility are at the heart of this work. The new sciences of Neuroplasticity, Neuroscience, Epigenetics, Positive Psychology, Quantum Physics and the Heart Brain Connection help to inform and provide a platform for the unique tools and techniques that, when practiced, consistently create an accountability culture that is life-changing for leaders, their teams, and their organizations as a whole. Creating capacity, improved productivity, and profits in our organizations will be grounded in a full understanding of what it is to be human and our ability to access all of the gifts and talents that this encompasses.

Keywords

Accountability Culture, Business Leadership, Emotional Intelligence, Heart Brain Connection, Human Capacity, Human Resources, Leadership, Leadership Development, Life Changing Leadership, Neuroplasticity, Neuroscience, Organizational Development, Purpose Driven Organizations, Science of Leadership, Spirituality of Leadership

Contents

Prologue

Life is funny. After 30 years of searching for what I believed would be a magical solution to the fear and stress associated with so many people's working lives, I now know there is no silver bullet and that it will always be evolving. The human being is an evolving species and as such we can only expect to see evolution in our businesses and schools worldwide as we seek better and more humane ways of interacting. The entire premise of science is to uncover new and wonderful things about our world and those that inhabit it so it stands to reason that as science uncovers new things about what it means to be human, we will utilize this new information to create better businesses, better working environments, and more meaningful ways of contributing.

When I first ventured out on my own and started Change Innovators Inc 15 years ago, I knew in the back of mind where I truly wanted to go. I had a gut feel where I would end up but, like all adventures, it unfolded in the most amazing and yet challenging ways. It has been a true journey of exploration and discovery as we created, revised, rebuilt, and envisioned our New World Leadership™ programming. We lost track several years ago which version of our program we were updating and simply surrendered to the fact that it would always be evolving. We realized our programming would need to change each and every year in order to stay ahead of the curve and to bring the newest information and science to the forefront of corporate life.

As the human being changes, grows, and evolves, we need to adjust our corporate environment to support those changes instead of continually forcing individuals to concede to the old way of doing things and the old energy rulebook. My experience is that organizations truly want their employees to be adaptable to constant change; however, these same organizations are often slow to adapt to the changing human who steps through their doors every day. I realize that it is a continuous moving target, yet corporations that adapt to the changing demographics of their contributors are the ones that will create the environment where optimal human performance can exist and, more importantly, thrive.

Creating The Accountability Culture: The Science of Life Changing Leadership is about this journey. At no time in recent history has the need for change been more obvious than today. This work is designed to openly share the journey of creating an environment where each and every employee truly wants to, and does, take full responsibility for the outcomes they get. The victim mentality is gone and the commitment to personal and organizational performance is evident everywhere.

We will explore some of the newest scientific discoveries relating to human performance as well as many topics we intuitively know simply because we are human. Many of us have forgotten how to tap into these innate skills and abilities that are part of being human. Through great questions and exploration, you will have an opportunity to evaluate for yourself what feels right and what does not. Some of the information in these pages will challenge your thinking right at the core. If you stay open and are willing to consider new ways of thinking and being at work, I believe you will have fun, learn, and possibly have a life changing experience. I realize this is a bold statement but I use it because our clients have stated this for many years. Don't take my word for it, experience it for yourself. My goal is to provide as much information as possible and give you, the leader or business owner, an opportunity to consider what might work in your world. If you have contributors that feel stuck, disempowered, where low engagement and the victim mentality thrives, you might just find some new tools within these pages to help make the big paradigm shift once and for all.

I do want to say that regardless of your views, good or bad, the shift to a culture of accountability is a journey of epic proportions but the ride is fun and the results amazing. The pathway is simple but the work is not easy. It requires a rewiring of the brain and a new connection to the heart, but once you have the necessary tools and techniques it becomes a true labor of love. The rewards are optimal performance, significant commitment, and an empowerment that has not been felt in corporate life in over 100 years.

I welcome your feedback and questions. As this work evolves and changes we rely on our readers and clients to help inform the work. If you have any questions, comments, or candid feedback, we want to know. I personally respond to all genuine inquiries so please feel free to e-mail me at ythompson@changeinnovators.com

Acknowledgments

This work is dedicated to the countless clients and hundreds of leaders who have had the courage to take the journey of New World Leadership™ and who are right now creating The Accountability Culture through their continued efforts. The joy we experience when we see a leader who is stuck in old energy thinking move to new energy openness full of compassion, love, and detachment makes every day we do this a true blessing. It has been our absolute pleasure to serve you and we look forward to bringing you the newest evolution in leadership each and every year. Thank you for trusting us with your valuable human resources and your continued support of this very important work.

A warm and heartfelt thank you to Lisa Fugard who diligently worked on the first round edit and to Caroline Mitic for taking my rough sketches of the models and imagines and creating the wonderful Accountability Model that we use each and every day with our clients.

PART I
Exploring Our Levels of Consciousness

CHAPTER 1

Let the Journey Begin

This is the most exciting time to be working in the corporate world and specifically in the field of leadership. Never before have we seen so much change, upheaval, new science, and shaky ground relating to the new direction of leadership in the business community. Nothing makes my heart sing like seeing a leader have that ah-ha light bulb moment where he or she connects the dots for the first time and realizes that he or she can turn ownership for results, accountability, and responsibility over to his or her team member who is actually doing the work. In fact, that is simply where the ownership belongs. The leader has made the necessary and important connections to both their logical brain and heart-centered emotions. There is meaningful alignment and balance between heart and head. They have the new and important skills to create the necessary environment where individual contributors simply want to be responsible and accountable for their outcomes and overall results. This is the sweet spot.

Creating the Accountability Culture: The Science of Life-changing Leadership is a compilation of many years of research and experience from the school of hard knocks. It details a formula and model that we have seen work over and over again. As the journey unfolds, leaders slowly become aware of how to create the right environment where amazing performance and true accountability can reside. I find nothing more rewarding than working with clients who openly admit that the old way no longer works. These clients have a genuine desire to make positive changes within their corporate culture. They recognize the significant stress people are under and they want to provide an environment where relief can occur. This relief creates an openness and curiosity, which results in increased exploration. We see capacity improve along with a renewed sense of sustainability, and then joy and happiness quickly follow. The journey is fabulous, tough at times but worth every moment, as we observe leaders transform from the old dense energy of command and control to a lighter more fluid energy of expression, commitment, accountability, and unparalleled focus on results. This occurs out of respect for the company and what it stands for, and not from a place of compliance.

The Accountability Model has evolved over the past 15 years of working with clients large and small. We have watched it unfold into a smooth process and unique journey for each and every leader. The process is fluid and flexible and becomes a road map that assists leaders in appreciating the human experience. Instead of resisting what it is to be human by demonstrating to employees how to ignore the natural human needs we all have, these leaders embrace it and allow others to do the same. The organization expects a lot from contributors, it is not about making friends and playing politics, it is about tapping into what it means to truly access all of the gifts and strengths of humanity within a corporate setting. We have been playing small, accessing only a portion of our brains and almost nothing from our hearts, thinking that if we are tough and work harder and harder we will win the race. Nothing could be farther from the truth.

The leader of the future plays only one key role. The leader creates the environment where others can and will take full responsibility and accountability for actions, behaviors, outcomes, and final results. This work is meaningful, engaging, and highly purpose driven. This is where true sustainable results exist and it is incredibly fun to play in this arena. Nothing could be more important in the coming years than to create an amazing culture where individual contributors love coming to work, feel connected to something meaningful, and go above and beyond for their work family and organization. Whoever said work shouldn't be fun, I suspect, was buried in density and heaviness. I hope you will come on this journey with me as we explore the many aspects of the new sciences combined with my version of spirituality that has become the foundation of the Accountability Model.

The Flow

Creating the Accountability Culture: The Science of Life-Changing Leadership is divided into two parts. These parts are very different and yet are so important to the building of an Accountability Culture. Part I is all about the foundation, the science, and the spiritual connections. Part II explores the tools and techniques of the Accountability Model and includes daily and weekly practices that assist leaders in their growth and evolution.

Without a really strong foundation, nothing will last. Many organizations think and sometimes say that they want the quick 10 steps to great leadership. A great example is when we are teaching our seven-month Coaching as a Leader program. Participants will often ask in Module III or Module IV, when are we going to get to the competencies and capabilities of great coaching? They have been programmed to get a checklist with the 'how to's. Why all the preparation? There is a very clear reason for this and a method to our madness.

If we want transformation, we must build a very strong foundation that includes understanding, clarity, and lots of opportunity for reflection before we venture into the core coaching capabilities. Many leaders have long-standing programming relating to what they believe a manager needs to do in order to get results. This programming must be rewritten. It is not for the faint of heart or for those that simply like command and control. The philosophy and process we use works best in companies who want unparalleled shift, results, and accountability and who are willing to dabble in the unknown from a corporate perspective. We explore purpose, compassion, truth, alignment, neuroscience, neurochemistry, and magnetic energy fields, and create a new framework for examining the human as leader. It takes courage, commitment, and a lot of love to make the shift but once you do it, it will be like opening yourself up to the most incredible fresh air where abundance, resources, and well-being in all of its forms can exist. Joy and passion can emerge organically and easily within all contributors. I encourage you to stay with Part I even when you think, wow this is a lot of information and citations, are we ever going to get to the process and Accountability Model? The foundation is important.

Part II of the book is the practical application. It completes the circle including real examples and the process that we have seen work over and over again. When reading about some of the concepts in Part II you may simply say, "No way, that is ridiculous we could never do that." However, it is essential to creating sustainable corporations of the future, corporations where people want to join your team and work their butts off to help make the company successful. They do this from a true place of alignment and commitment, not from a place of compliance. You will be able to attract the best talent that is intellectual, innovative, focused, and truly committed from a place of honesty, love, and passion.

When I made the decision to write this book, I was nervous about how I could take something that is so internal, soul felt, and so personally experienced and put it into words where others could *feel* the intent and process. Our clients have been telling us for years that the process and results are life changing for themselves, their team, and their organization. This book is as much about *feeling* the material as intellectualizing it, so I encourage you to stay open, be curious, and be willing to dive deep into the concepts. Be willing to consider that what we are doing today is not sustainable and that a completely new approach is needed if we are going to create amazing companies where people truly want to be, where work doesn't feel like work but feels like an honor, a commitment, and a soul-felt journey of contribution.

Definitions

The following section provides some basic background and definitions that will assist you in working through the material. Some of the words I have chosen as key descriptors might not resonate with you in the way I have intended them. I felt it was important to provide some context. For example, the word spirituality invokes all kinds of emotions and thoughts. My use of the word is very intentional as it represents what it is to be human. If I was to say that we are logical beings with an intellect, a left and right brain hemisphere, no one is likely to dispute that. But when I say we are spiritual beings and that our humanness is about recognizing our emotions, connecting to the heart center, and understanding some basic innate needs, we might have some debate. Spirituality for the purposes of this book is about recognizing that we are complex beings that are mostly emotional and partially logical. These two parts within all of us work closely together and if we don't take a holistic approach to the overall complexities of being human, we miss valuable information that informs our leadership role and corporate world. Here are the definitions that I think will assist in navigating the material.

The Accountability Model

This is the name given to the model created by Change Innovators Inc which is shared with their permission. The model provides the reader with a visual of the tools, process, and techniques used in order to create a culture where each and every contributor can take 100 percent responsibility for their actions and the outcomes they get. It is important to acknowledge that this is *not* about the leader holding people accountable. This model is about creating a context and an environment where every contributor wants to personally hold themselves accountable to the outcomes they get.

Compelling Purpose

The term *compelling purpose* is used in the context of organizational life, to describe *why* a business is in business. An organization's compelling purpose is different from the traditional mission and vision statement. It is intrinsic, internal, and felt, instead of something that is intellectualized. I dedicate a full section to this topic.

Emotional Intelligence

Emotional intelligence is the regulation of emotions and the healthy, positive use of emotions in order to increase personal and professional effectiveness. It is also defined as the ability to use the information provided by emotions to act appropriately in the face of challenges.

Energy

I use the word *energy* a lot within these pages. A formal and traditional definition of energy is shared in a subsequent chapter; however, for now my use of this word is intended to mean those things we can feel but not necessarily see. It is the transference of feelings amongst individuals that is not spoken but felt and that has impact, either intended or unintended. It can be felt individually or collectively based on whether we are working with an individual leader or a team or group of people. I also reference the magnetic energy field that surrounds each of us.

Heart Brain

We will also discuss and use the term heart brain. In 1991, Dr. J. Andrew Armour first introduced the term *heart brain*. He discovered that the heart has a complex nervous system. In some scientific circles this complex nervous system qualifies as a brain because of the way it operates. The HeartMath Institute™ has studied the science of the heart for over 14 years and they have proven that the heart has an intricate network of neurons, neurotransmitters, proteins, and support cells. "This results in the heart's ability to act independently, to learn, remember, feel, and sense" (HeartMath Institute 2016).

Heart Centered

Heart centered is a term used when a person accesses their intuitive inner voice. The gut feeling that lets a person know they are on the right track. It is when things *feel* right. We often refer to the left brain as being the portion of the brain that assists us with logical evidence-based thinking, process, and structure, while the right brain assists with creativity, innovation, and bigger picture thinking. The heart center, when properly utilized, lets us know when things *feel* right or *feel* wrong. When we go deep inside and seek our personal truth, our heart center guides us if we are willing to listen carefully and quietly.

Love

I use the word *love* to describe the deep caring that leaders have for one another and for their team members. It is a connection to the heart center that is felt in a genuine way. It is the recognition of our commonalities that binds us together. For example, many people feel that parting ways with employees is so difficult and feels so uncomfortable. In the New Energy Organization, where accountability flourishes, parting ways usually comes from a place of understanding, love, and compassion. The leader's intentions come from a very good place and they know that all parties will be better off in the future. It is a true gift.

Neuroplasticity

A term used to describe the ability of the brain to make new neural connections and new brain cells. A term used in the field of neuroscience.

New Energy Organization

An organization that recognizes employees want opportunities for responsible self-management; one that focuses on creating positive energy using the newest information in positive psychology, neuroplasticity, and heart or brain connection. An organization that creates a culture where accountability flourishes.

New World Leadership™ and Spiritually Aligned Leadership™

I will refer to New World Leadership™ (NWL) when speaking about the leadership training philosophy, leadership programming, and the new state of our world as it relates to business leadership. Spiritually Aligned Leadership™ is usually referenced when speaking about a leader's personal journey, the process of seeking one's personal truth and alignment. These terms are sometimes used interchangeably. However, The New World Leadership™ Series is the formal name of the leadership program that this work is based on. It is used with permission from Change Innovators® (Change Innovators Inc. 2017), the organization that owns all of the intellectual property related to this program. Spiritually Aligned Leadership™ is a way of being.

Old Energy Organization

A traditional command and control culture where employees feel disempowered and the victim mentality is unintentionally promoted.

Organic Influence

This is a natural result when a person practices the tools and techniques described in this work. It occurs over time in a very subtle but powerful way. If you are a Spiritually Aligned Leader, others just want to be around you; they want what you have. They want to follow you and to understand what you practice. Organic Influence is when people are drawn to a leader because they create positive energy everywhere they go. They do not become unbalanced easily and they self-correct all of the time. They are consistent, fair, and completely open to everyone and their views. They have faith in themselves, in others, and in the larger world around them. Interactions with others are *always* positive. This doesn't mean they don't have challenges or obstacles in their lives (although they may have fewer), but it is about how they navigate those obstacles that matters. In fact, obstacles are really not obstacles to the Spiritually Aligned Leader, they are opportunities. People witness their balanced and positive approach to adversity and they want to know how the leader does it. This is *Organic Influence*. It is created with *no* egoic intent, meaning that ego is not involved; it is simply the way the person is. Others want to follow out of a true desire to feel that same balance and alignment.

Roommate or Noise

I will use the term *roommate* or *noise* interchangeably. This term refers to the conversations you have in your head with yourself or with your "Roommate." It is the continuous *noise* we have going on up there. It can be the undesirable internal dialogue with the roommate.

Spiritual Alignment

I intend no religious connotations when I use this term. It is not my intention, in any way, to challenge anyone's religious beliefs. I strongly value diversity and a person's right to choose his or her own direction in life and this is in fact at the core of our work. Each individual person needs to seek and follow his or her own truth. Spiritual alignment simply means that a leader has tapped into his or her heart center and has found his or her true alignment. Spiritual alignment is when a leader aligns mind, body, and spirit; meaning that they value and utilize the heart centered (heart brain), gut feeling, and internal guidance system in alignment with their left or right brain. They understand when the ego is in play and manage it appropriately. I often refer to spirituality as the important relationship one has with themselves. One of my colleagues describes it as complete acceptance of others and, through this process, the individual becomes completely accepting of self.

We

You will notice that I often refer to "we" at various points throughout the book. I do this to acknowledge the team I have worked with at Change Innovators Inc®. Many of the concepts and philosophies presented here have been developed over years as part of The New World Leadership™ program. It is with permission and gratitude that I share their work.

Final Thoughts Before We Begin the Real Journey

I believe the only way to change organizational life in a positive way is to assist one leader at a time to connect with their true self and all that this encompasses. The heart center never lies and we intuitively know this to be true. There is nothing easy about this work as it takes significant courage and commitment. The results are astounding. At a time when businesses are desperately seeking cost-effective ways to improve performance and overall business results with less resources, what have we got to lose? Is it possible we will discover something that has been missing in corporate life for over 100 years? We might discover the true power that lies within each of us. It is time for all leaders to challenge themselves to tap into their true nature, seek their personal alignment, and to use this true nature to create positive energy. This positive energy creates the right context for the leader to practice the specific tools and techniques of the Accountability Model that, in turn, produces amazing results that are life changing in all of its forms.

CHAPTER 2

Old Energy Organizations

As human beings we seem to be forever creating lists or statements that say what we will *do*. We articulate objectives, goals, and future visions and yet we rarely know how to *be*. *Being* is different from *doing*. *Being* is an internal state of knowing, with clear honest intention and a sense of alignment. *Doing* is about getting stuff done and it rarely aligns with an internalized state of being. Old energy organizations are almost always focused on *doing* with little sense of what is means to simply *be*. This chapter explores the many attributes of old energy organizations and how these attributes have impacted human behavior and our ability to be high-performing leaders who organically create high performing teams.

Fear-Based Management

Many of us have heard the statement that there are fundamentally only two core emotions, love and fear, and that all other emotions stem from these two core emotions. Best-selling author Marianne Williamson speaks of this often in her work. It is evident in organizational life as well, within teams and with individual contributors.

We might be able to extrapolate that the emotion of fear present in organizational life arises out of societal norms and beliefs that originated in child-rearing practices of times gone by:

- Respect your elders, police, and educators, regardless of whether it is earned.
- To succeed, you need to compete and be the best.
- Working hard and demonstrating you will always go above and beyond will get you further.

- Winning and the accumulation of wealth is what matters. This sense of accumulation of wealth can also result in a hidden belief that there is not enough for everyone, so it is important to hoard what you have.

All of these old paradigms can be seen, and more importantly felt, in old energy organizations. They show up in the form of hoarding resources, competition among peers, and the need to respect the manager/supervisor regardless of how they lead. These practices and beliefs are not only outdated, but studies have proven that they do *not* facilitate performance. We will look closer at this in future chapters.

The majority of emotions exhibited in old energy organizations stem from a place of fear. Look at Table 2.1 and consider your organization. Do you believe that it is bound by *love* or bound by *fear*? Do employees feel safe, cared for, and honored? Can contributors truly be themselves at work? In situations where something goes wrong, do you look to the rulebook or policy to tell you what the right thing to do is?

In fear-based organizations, leaders continuously ask themselves, "What would my boss want?" We spend time trying to figure out the

Table 2.1 Love versus fear

Fear	Love
Anxiety	Compassion
Frustration	Gratitude/Appreciation
Lacking (there is never enough)	Abundance (there is enough)
Anger	Joy
Impatience	Patience
Suspicion	Trust
Competition	Creativity
Overwhelming	Balance/Alignment
Ego	Humility/Grace
Stuck–one way (the right way)	Open–mindedness
Speak what others want to hear	Honesty with good intention

expectations of our manager and how we can accomplish whatever we think will make him or her happy. We do this because we have learned from a very young age that life is easier when we follow, do as we are told, and fit in. In these old energy organizations, leaders believe individual contributors would not know what to do if they didn't tell them. If we peel away the layers of the onion, we might discover that there is a belief that frontline contributors are not capable of good decision making and thoughtful analysis. In some situations, leaders simply like control and power so there is little consideration given to allowing contributors to be involved in important decision making. However, often the leader still wants to hold the employee accountable.

Most experiences in our formative years led us to believe that fitting in and following a set of rigid rules was advantageous. When we get our first job we discover that if you do what you are told, you will fit in and get along. Life will be easier. You will always have a paycheck. Beneath all of these examples is fear: the fear of not fitting in, the fear of the consequences of being different, of sharing our true thoughts and feelings, the fear of losing the ever-important paycheck, fear of being judged. It is no wonder that when we get our first leadership opportunity we expect people to do what they are told. We expect them to get along and fit in, and we begin to believe that anyone who does not make an effort to do this is not a team player.

Questions are always more important than answers. Questions allow us to reflect and consider. The question that comes to mind here is this: Does this old energy approach facilitate creativity, innovation, risk taking, and entrepreneurial efforts?

Understanding Our Filters

Human beings have a number of filters that impact how we see the world. The filters begin at a very early age and are taught to us by our parents, clergy, teachers, and employers. A simple example of a filter that might be developed over time, is that only those that do well in school will do well in business and in life. As our parents and schools taught us this, we began to believe it and so it became a filter shading us from the possibility that there could be another truth. In fact, there have been many people throughout history that were extremely successful without a postsecondary education. Research conducted at Stanford University by Charles O'Reilly and Jennifer Chatman also concluded that high Graduate Management Admission Test (GMAT) scores were an insufficient predictor of success (O'Reilly and Chatman 1994, p. 603). One of the more profound results of this limited thinking is that old energy organizations have built strong paradigms on the premise that using the left brain, process-driven, cognitive thinking is the most important factor leading to business success. In today's incredibly fast-paced environment, this thinking can be very limiting. Old energy organizations can rely so heavily on the cognitive knowledge of their leaders that they miss other critical information that is available to them.

Another filter that might occur is one relating to gender. Women can learn from their family dynamic that they are the best childcare providers and that men should be the primary income earners. If we were raised in this environment, this may become our truth and a filter is applied, one that shades us from other possibilities.

We create filters in society that say we must be hard working, we must go to university, we must fit into the corporate dogma, we must make a certain income and have certain possessions to be deemed successful. One of the most common and general filters is the belief that there is good and bad behavior and that we need to fit into a specific mold in order to be successful in life.

All of these filters block our vision to other possibilities. In future chapters we will look at the neuroscience of belief, but suffice to say here that what we believe is what we focus on to the exclusion of so many other possibilities. Filters vary from country to country and from culture to culture. All you have to do is travel to a third-world country or watch well-researched documentaries on success and happiness and you will find that many people with very few personal possessions, in comparison to the western world, believe themselves to be successful and extremely happy.

The key is to cultivate the awareness that filters can block our sight and senses to other possibilities, thus limiting our worldview. Beliefs can become so strong that they can ultimately affect outcomes against all odds. An interesting example of this is a study conducted in 2006 in

Canada, which included 220 female students. These students were given fake research reports claiming that men had a 5-percent advantage over women in math performance (Dar-Nimrod and Heine 2006, p. 435). The women were divided into two groups. One group was given specific information that the results were based on genetic factors. The second group was told that the results were due to the way teachers stereotype girls and boys in elementary school. The subjects were then given the exact same math test. Those that were told the lower scores were due to a genetic disadvantage scored lower than those told it was due to stereotyping in schools. They concluded that those that truly believed they had a genetic disadvantage performed as if they truly were disadvantaged. Our thoughts and beliefs are powerful tools affecting our lives in a myriad of ways.

The goal in considering our filters is to reflect on how significantly our world is changing day by day and how much harder it is becoming to perform under the old dogma. Many old energy leaders believe that the world would be better if we all agreed on a clear set of rules and procedures. Filters can become so strong they can shade a leader's vision from numerous possibilities, leading them to believe that only their limited view of a situation is correct. How many possibilities are available to us and yet never exposed? Many of the leaders we work with are deeply stuck having strongly ingrained beliefs; they simply can't imagine a new and different work environment. Usually we see a density of ingrained filters in older energy organizations, which often create very low engagement and high stress levels due to a sense of personal misalignment. We also see slow reaction time to issues or overreaction to issues in order to simply control the environment and get back to a so-called normal state, because anything other than this is frightening.

The Death of Creativity—The Drudgery of Work?

The old energy environment is anything but inspiring, joyful, collaborative, and connected. It is founded in routine, compliance, order and a *tell* or *instruct* mentality. Many organizations have been known at one time or another to state, "Work is work and you should not bring your personal life to the business." This statement tells people to leave a part of themselves at home, in particular the emotional part. What are leaders afraid of? What are old energy organizations hiding from? At the core of these organizations is a lack of understanding of the depth and complexity of the emotional human being and the connection to behaviors and outcomes. They have been trying to take a complex human being and fit them into a simple model of command and control.

Most organizations didn't start off saying, I want employees to fear us and our authority. If we reflect on the early beginnings, we see creative, inspirational entrepreneurs with a vision and a passion for something they believed in. But as an organization grows, so can the fear and we begin to build rigid structure in hopes of keeping control. Over time, through our complex policies, rulebook and mechanistic approach to conflict and change, we stifle creativity, decision making, and the use of intuition.

Many organizations have been trying to soften this approach; however, the old energy approaches are so ingrained in leaders (hard wired) that the shift is incredibly difficult. Old energy organizations have focused on the bottom two rungs of Maslow's Hierarchy of Needs (McLeod 2016) for over 100 years; the fear of loss of income, which directly relates to food, water, and shelter, is often an underlying current in old energy organizations. This might seem very dramatic, but if we really think about ourselves and our colleagues, we will discover that fear has been a part of our working lives for as long as we have been gathering in formal workplaces. We have learned to settle, with very low expectations of our employers. The times we *had* higher expectations we were often let down. This is because most organizations have spent very little time nurturing and creating a context where love, friendship, esteem, and self-actualization can occur. How can we ever get the best performance when we use mechanisms that only focus on a very small part of what it means to be human? The old carrot and stick routine is simply that: *old*.

I love to share this message which was posted in a Canadian newspaper many years ago and given to me by a delegate at a conference. It speaks volumes about where we have been in our organizational lives. Unfortunately, I am unable to provide the original credit as it was simply handed to me as a small cutout from a newspaper.

Bank Rules for Staff 1878

1. Godliness, cleanliness, and punctuality are the necessities of a good business.
2. This firm has reduced the hours of work, and the clerical staff will now only have to be present between the hours of 7 am and 6 pm on weekdays.
3. Daily prayers will be held each morning in the main office. The clerical staff will be present.
4. Clothing must be of a sober nature. The clerical staff will not disport themselves in raiment of bright colors, nor will they wear hose, unless in good repair. Overshoes and topcoats may not be worn in the office, but neck scarves and headwear may be worn in inclement weather.
5. A stove is provided for the benefit of clerical staff. Coal and wood must be kept in the locker, it is recommended that each member of the clerical staff bring four pounds of coal each day during the cold weather.
6. No member of the clerical staff may leave the room without permission from Mr. Rogers. The calls of nature are permitted and clerical staff may use the garden below the second gate. This area must be kept in good order.
7. No talking is allowed during business hours.
8. The craving of tobacco, wines, and spirits is a human weakness and as such, is forbidden to all members of the clerical staff.
9. The owners recognize the new Labor Laws, but will expect a great rise in output of work to compensate for the near Utopian conditions (Dominion Bank Rules Unknown).

I realize how dramatic the above may appear, but imagine what it was like to work within the culture created by this environment. I suspect that many organizations of that period had similar rules and beliefs about how to control and manage their contributors, better known by the term "staff." This is where we evolved from, these are the roots of old energy. For a moment ignore the specific rules and think about how the overall message *feels*. What emotions does it invoke? Does it possibly invoke feelings of restriction and lack of control, maybe even fear? *What if I don't follow the rules?*

Human beings are a complex species with many different attributes. You will probably acknowledge that emotions play a significant role in how we interact and react to rules. Emotions displayed through words and actions are critical to the success of the individual leader and in turn, their team. Fear and its subemotions often produce an inability to make clear decisions; it holds us back from creativity and innovation. This is so important when we consider productivity. In subsequent chapters we will discuss the connections between how a person *feels* and their ability to perform and we will take a look at the newest sciences informing the field of leadership.

I recognize that organizational life has dramatically changed and that employees have a much more flexible work environment with significantly improved benefits. But if we asked them how they feel within their workplaces, what do you think the answer would be? Have things really changed that much?

Many old energy organizations are providing more extrinsic rewards, such as money, benefits, and gifts, in an effort to improve motivation and, ultimately, performance. Research shows this does not improve performance, especially in our more complex work environments where critical decision making is frequently required. Studies have shown that it is the intrinsic rewards that make a difference; how persons *feel* about their work and their overall contribution to something bigger than themselves is very important and directly connected to performance. Thomas G. Crane, author of *The Heart of Coaching*, describes the research conducted by Glenn Tobe & Associates that resulted in a list of the top 10 motivators for employees as compared to what managers thought were the top 10 motivators for employees (Crane 2012, p. 28). The differences are quite astounding. For example, employees stated that appreciation, feeling "in" on things, an understanding attitude, and job security were the top four motivators. While the managers believed that employees, top motivators were good wages, job security, promotion opportunities, and good working conditions.

What's Missing?

Old energy organizations rely on left-brain, evidence-based, logical analysis for decision making. Rarely will a leader ask, "What does your intuition tell you or what does your gut say on this issue?" It has only been in the last 15 years that there has been active dialogue around creativity and innovation (right brain). People have been awakening to the idea that right-brain thinking is advantageous for business and that creative debate is an instrumental tool to good decision making. Organizations like Apple and Facebook have made it okay to think, act, and behave creatively when it comes to business. But let's be really honest here: How many organizations talk about creativity, brainstorming, and out-of-the-box thinking, but then stifle the creativity when it comes down to the actual decision making? Often there are only a few people at the top making the decisions for the entire organization. Real creativity and dynamic decision making is often nonexistent, especially below a manager level. My experience is that even managers are merely implementing decisions made by others. We don't tap into the intellect of mainstream contributors. Old energy organizations value and honor left-brain capacity and sometimes right-brain, but rarely heart-centered intuition.

It is not hard to understand why organizational life still does not operate at optimal levels when we encourage the human being to only bring part of him or herself into the workplace. If it helps to understand Figure 2.1, you can replace the word "spirit" with emotions or feelings or heart center. Regardless of what we call it, we have been encouraged, for some time now, not to bring the fullness of what it is to be human into the workplace. It is like saying to the carpenter, please bring your hammer and nails, but do not bring the saw. If an employee leaves a portion of who they are at home, they cut themselves off from important innate, natural skills that have been proven to aid in decision making and clarity. They suppress these important innate abilities and as a result create

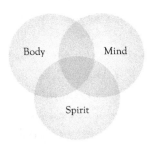

Figure 2.1 Body Mind Spirit

personal misalignment. I like to ask a simple question of those I coach, "Have you ever made a decision that you knew you shouldn't make, but you made it anyway? How did you know you shouldn't have made it?" Most will say, "I had a gut feeling, my intuition was telling me."

This unwillingness to truly accept that the human being is more complex and can bring more to work than simply their brain or their body is hurting organizational performance, not to mention the health and well-being of the individual contributor.

Are We Still Lying?

Old energy organizations ultimately create a go-along to get-along mentality where often employees and leaders alike do not speak their mind at meetings and hold back what they believe to be true on issues. In many old energy organizations, we will hear things like, "this is a need-to-know basis." Senior leaders who use this approach often don't realize that this practice in itself is based in fear. *What if people find out before we are ready to answer their questions? What if people are unhappy with the decision and decide not to support it?* At the core of this practice is a belief that frontline employees will not be able to handle the truth. I am not suggesting that there is not a place for holding back information, especially when protecting someone's privacy or the closing of a crucial deal with legal requirements; however, this practice is used much more frequently than necessary. My experience with this approach is that often the frontline employees already have a good idea of what is going to happen. They can tell there is another change in the air and the withholding of information creates more fear and unrest. It also increases the lack of trust.

An example would be that you are not to discuss an issue or problem with anyone above your own boss. Jumping the queue or lines of authority is considered a huge infraction. Why do organizations create these rules? Consider all the reasons this is done and then ask yourself: Are the reasons based in love or fear? What emotions are connected to these written and sometimes unwritten rules? Is it an open and collaborative system based on honesty or a closed system based on authority and imposed respect? Does this come from an old filter of respect your elders or respect your boss regardless of their action? This is how important issues are driven underground as employees don't feel there is anywhere to turn. Honesty goes hand in hand with trust. We will discuss in future chapters how to create a trusting environment.

Ego

Ego is still a major player in old energy organizations. It creates a culture based on a need to win, a need to be right, and a need to have things unfold based on a small group of leaders' viewpoints. The filters created in childhood, as mentioned earlier in this chapter, and the fear factor created by our environments, have left us disconnected from our spiritual selves. We have dialed down our intuitive internal guidance. The more disconnected we are from our true alignment, the more our ego plays into how we lead. We begin to think we know what is best for others, especially within the work environment.

When a senior leader makes a decision with little or no consultation that affects a mid-level leader and his or her area of responsibility, the mid-level leader can feel the loss of collaboration and control. If this happens repeatedly, the loss of control is very unsettling. The mid-level leader feels underutilized, uninvolved, and left out of important decision making. They learn through their experiences firsthand and so they too begin to model this same behavior, even if their intuition tells them this is not the best way to lead. These mid-level leaders begin to make decisions for their supervisors with little or no consultation. This ripple effect occurs because, as human beings, we need to feel a sense of mastery over our day. That does not mean that we have to get everything our own way, but we do need to feel that basic decisions regarding our day are within our control.

Human beings want to belong and contribute. But in old energy organizations a leader will take whatever control he or she can get. This is never healthy and often results in elevated egos for everyone; each trying to find their place where they can have a little bit of control. In such an environment there is no place for collaboration and a true sense of open-minded contribution.

One of my favorite quotes comes from Dr. Carl Jung who stated, "Healing comes only from that which leads the patient beyond himself and beyond his entanglements with ego" (Crane 2012, p. 154). Negotiating with our ego is a key skill for leaders today and the Accountability Model shared in Part II of this book helps us accomplish this.

Separation

One of the more common attributes of old energy organizations is a sense of separation. What does this mean? It means that we see individuals as separate from the whole. There is a lack of true understanding of collective energy and how systems work. Old energy organizations spend a lot of time working on and with individual contributors instead of working from a place of collective purpose and team alignment. The word energy is rarely used, if ever, in these organizations and there is fear that if we don't manage individual performance we will remove the importance of individual accountability. The leaders in these organizations are unintentionally trained to see separation to the exclusion of the collective. This concept will be expanded on in a subsequent chapter.

Performance Management

Old energy organizations are based on a very old mechanistic viewpoint that states our role is to manage people and their performance. An important question to ask is: Can we really manage (control) the performance of another person? There is incredible richness in this question. Most people struggle to manage their own performance, behavior, attitudes, emotions, and outcomes and the belief that we can actually manage that of someone else seems ludicrous. As we begin to understand human behavior, we realize that many of our ingrained beliefs set us up for failure and do not provide any real benefit in helping us manage performance.

Often the management team is at the center of everything and the employees are simply there to get stuff done as directed by the leader. Managers believe there is a wrong way and right way. Managers try to manage how employees act, perform, contribute, and behave and yet they actually have little or no control over this. From these beliefs emerge rigid performance management programs. Many organizations will train managers and supervisors on how to implement their performance management and discipline policies, but will not provide them with progressive leadership exploration and opportunities for education in this area. Moving an employee from a plant floor operator on Friday to a supervisor of the operators on Monday still exists in many organizations. We promote the best welder to be the supervisor of the welders and expect them to manage the performance of others.

When we ask managers how they feel about their performance management programs, they tell us the programs are time consuming and often create more separation and isolation and do not actually improve performance.

Summary

Old energy organizations are entrenched in outdated systems of command and control and authority. The leadership of an old energy organization might define success as money, profitability, status, material possessions, market share, and the size of the organization. While new energy organizations do attain success, profits and market share is not their sole criteria for success and they define themselves quite differently. We will explore new energy organizations in the following chapter.

Our world has dramatically changed since organizational life began. I respect that organizations don't fall squarely into either old energy or new energy. Even within old energy organizations there are areas or departments of new energy. I also concede that some of my language is strong and my positions overemphasized, but I have experienced these extremes within my practice. We have made some progress since the Bank Rules of 1878, however we have a long way to go to fundamentally change the culture of organizational life. We cannot use old energy process to engage new energy employees. If we want to do more with less and create amazing results now and into the future, we need to move away from these traditional old energy mechanistic approaches.

CHAPTER 3

New Energy Organizations

As referenced in Chapter 2, understanding the difference between *doing and being* is critical to the new energy organization. New energy organizations understand that true alignment comes when this important and delicate balance is present. When employees are in personal and professional alignment they utilize significantly less effort and create more; that careful balance between *doing* and *being*. There is less conflict, more harmony, and much more collaboration where teams truly see and feel the value of working together. Discretionary effort is everywhere.

Successful employees in a new energy organization might be described as those who are balanced, have the freedom to be themselves, are emotionally intelligent and compassionate, and are in true alignment within themselves and with their organization's compelling purpose. Self-actualization is possible. What is fascinating to me is that as contributors awaken they truly believe that they can create balance within themselves and with their organization. This is why we see so much movement of our talent between organizations. It is not because the employee is fickle. It is because often the person is simply seeking an organization with which they can align, one with a compelling purpose that speaks to them.

Compelling Purpose

Most of us grew up believing that everything originates in the brain. All thoughts, talents, and information come from the left and right hemispheres. However, many very talented poets, musicians, dancers, and writers have said that their gift comes from an innate place deep within themselves. I believe that many very successful entrepreneurs feel the same way, that their gift, their talent, their drive to do something special come from a *knowing* deep inside. This calling, this search for meaning, is directly connected to an organization's compelling purpose.

Unfortunately most leadership experts still address a company's *raison d'être*[1] or reason for being in terms of vision and mission. But a compelling purpose is very different from the company's vision and mission statement. First, most vision and mission statements reference the customer or end user of the products or services. Second, a vision and mission statement is often connected to sales. It is designed and framed and usually posted on the wall and given a place of prominence on websites and in corporate literature. It often feels like a marketing campaign.

The difference between mission and vision statements and a compelling purpose can easily be understood through the lens of doing and being. A mission statement focuses on what the organization endeavors to do and the vision statement describes how the company sees itself in the future. Both are about *doing*. A compelling purpose will never need to be posted on the wall precisely because it is intrinsic to the organization and the organizational culture and its people. The compelling purpose is about *being*, it's effortless and needs no doctrine for it to be understood.

I have chosen the word *compelling* for a specific reason: People in the organization feel compelled to engage, to follow, with a true connection to the purpose. It is at the core of the organization, and highly valued. The compelling purpose is the connection to the emotional, intuitive, spiritual part of being human, that part that creates community and impacts the overall environment.

The compelling purpose is felt, lived, and internalized. It is ingrained in everything a new energy organization does. The compelling purpose connects to the contributors in a meaningful way and inspires and informs decisions. Contributors feel it internally and know that they are a part of something bigger than themselves. In new energy organizations, contributors choose to be a part of the organization because their compelling purpose is not simply a paycheck.

The size and impact of the compelling purpose is not what is important. What matters is that you identify with it, embrace it, and live it. The compelling purpose is the union between a person and the cause that has the momentum to produce great change in the world. Individuals with a

---

[1] *Raison d'être* is a phrase borrowed from French that means "reason for being."

compelling purpose include Mother Teresa, Martin Luther King Jr., and Rosa Parks.

So it is with new energy organizations. These organizations recognize that regardless of whether their compelling purpose is big or small, it is at the core of everything they do. The organizational values, decision making, and structure all reflect the compelling purpose. It is at the heart of who they are and why they exist.

The Edelman Goodpurpose® 2012 study provides valuable information gathered directly from over 8,000 consumers in 16 different markets about global consumer attitudes on social purpose, commitment, and brand expectations. Consumers worldwide are very clear regarding their expectations of corporate purpose and it turns out it is far more than the old-established Corporate Social Responsibility (CSR). It is about a clear definable purpose that includes a powerful integrated strategy with honest intent and long-term positive impact. Edelman states:

> Within 24/7 connectivity, hyper transparency and diminishing competitive barriers, companies and brands need a new narrative to break through the noise—something compelling that inspires stakeholders to engage, activate and advocate for an organization, beyond CSR, cause marketing and altruism. Purpose is a core strategy for profit and growth based on linking an organization's reason for being to improving lives and impacting society. (Edelman 2012)

As the Edelman Goodpurpose® study is conducted year over year, there is clear evidence that global consumers believe brands should support good causes and make money at the same time. In fact, making money allows them to support more good causes and not just returns to shareholders. From 2008 to 2012, there has been a 33-percent increase in this belief globally (Edelman 2012). Consumers are not only making purchasing decisions based on *purpose* they are in fact advocating for this.

Some organizations are created out of a core purpose that is deeply meaningful to the founder. In these instances, the compelling purpose creates a natural and organic recruitment process and attracts those who align with it. A compelling purpose often has significant longevity, although it can change form and direction over time.

A good example is Patagonia, founded by Yvon Chouinard, who wrote *Let My People Go Surfing: The education of a reluctant businessman* (Chouinard 2006). As I read the book, I could feel the enormous love Yvon had for mountain climbing, his passion for fishing and the outdoors. Pictures in the book show him sleeping under a tarp in a sleeping bag on the side of a mountain, without even a tent. He looks content and happy, as if he were truly living his purpose. He started his first company, the Chouinard Equipment Company, that focused specifically on mountain-climbing equipment. Slowly over time this organization became the Patagonia we know today, a very successful outdoor sports equipment and clothing company.

But what really happened here? I believe Yvon Chouinard's passion for the outdoors, his connection with nature, the environment, and a world larger than himself morphed into a business enterprise, a corporation. I believe the company grew because the people attracted to the company were drawn to its compelling purpose. Patagonia attracted men and women who honored and cared for the outdoors, who lived like this naturally, who chose this as a philosophy and way of life rather than as simply a place to work.

Patagonia remains driven by their compelling purpose, not only to make quality outerwear but to build sustainability and renewability into all of their practices (Patagonia 2017). When you visit their website you will quickly see all of their environmental initiatives: to choose vendors using strict criteria, to ensure that their environmental impact is minimal, to work toward renewability and sustainability. They also personally and financially support environmental causes.

This company is not alone. We are seeing more and more new energy organizations with a compelling purpose at the core of everything they do. A key factor is that the compelling purpose does not fade or waiver, even when times are difficult or when it is not convenient to do so. A compelling purpose defines who you are and why you exist, especially in the tough times. Consider Southwest Airlines, famous for its connection to being bound by love where employees are the first customers and guests on the plane are the number two customers (ChartHouse Learning 2001). What does that tell you about this company? My sense is that the compelling purpose of this organization, as stated in the video *It's So Simple,* is to love what they do and each other and to pass that love onto their customers.

A friend I know well works for Unilever. I noticed on her Facebook page a reference to loving the company she works for. What fabulous advertising! Who needs a marketing department when you have employees who freely and openly speak highly of their organization?

As recently reported by *Fortune,* Unilever has a clear purpose, with three very ambitious goals. It is focused on helping over a billion people around the world to improve health and well-being. It is working to reduce the environmental footprint of their products by 50 percent and to secure their agricultural raw materials from sustainable sources. To create a culture that is truly focused on a core purpose takes intentional commitment and a true desire to make a difference. Since Paul Polman took over as CEO, the organization's employee engagement scores have improved by 12 percent. As noted in *Fortune,*

> When LinkedIn unveiled its data-fueled list of the most sought-after employers in the world, a few months ago, the companies at the very top of the heap came as no surprise: Google, followed by Apple. But coming in at No. 3—ahead of Microsoft and Facebook— was a very different breed of business: consumer-products giant Unilever, whose Dutch roots stretch back more than 140 years. (Wartzman 2015)

I wonder if the CEO of Unilever wants employees and shareholders alike to connect to the compelling purpose so that he can build momentum and positive energy. Does he intuitively know that when we get a large group of people focused on an important and meaningful purpose we can create significant change and significant results? Maybe he does and maybe he doesn't but for me the real important question here is: Can we change outcomes using conscious deliberate positive energy? Does consciousness have energy? I believe the answer is *yes.* I will share some recent research and further information on this topic in a subsequent chapter.

Leadership Development

One of my observations over the past five years is that although there is a significant amount of stress and anxiety within our organizations, there is also something very positive and profound happening. Many leaders are awakening to their spiritual nature. They are doing their personal work and asking themselves the difficult questions about who they are and who they want to be. They are seeking to self-balance, to remove the victim mentality, and to build self-empowerment from the inside out. This gives us so much to be optimistic about. As our frontline contributors and leaders alike evolve, so must our organizations. Like the tipping point, it is only a matter of time.

New energy organizations understand that at the core of any successful company is leadership, personal development, and an inward focus on alignment. The key is to understand what kind of leadership will be most successful in today's context. In these organizations there is a conscious choice to promote people who truly live the compelling purpose of the organization. These leaders understand the importance of being self-centered and self-focused; they know that when they *lead self* they will create organic influence that has long-term positive impact. They model the way for others. These leaders understand that the only way to change the outer world is to change their inner world first. They are consistent. Not perfect, but consistently working on their stuff in order to be the best they can be. They monitor ego at every stage of decision making. This is critical because when leaders are not working on themselves, when they are on autopilot simply reacting to situations and people, everyone around them knows it.

Here is another important quotation used in the New World Leadership programming. "Leadership has everything to do with you the leader and nothing to do with you at the same time" (Change Innovators Inc. 2017). I would ask you to reflect on this as we move through subsequent chapters. What does it mean to you and how does it apply in your leadership role? This contradiction should become clear as we unpack the tools and techniques to creating the New World Leader and The Accountability Culture.

Leading with Love and Compassion

At the core of new energy organizations is a belief that all employees have common needs and wants: They want to belong and need to have some control over their day, they want to contribute to something meaningful. At the same time leaders are aware that although there are commonalities, each person is unique and has their own gifts, liabilities, and perceptions of the world. A one-size-fits-all approach does not work.

New energy organizations do not rely heavily on the rulebook to guide their decision making but more often see it as a guideline that is used out of respect, not obligation. Leaders are given the freedom to make decisions as long as they align with the values and compelling purpose of the organization. This includes exploring each situation uniquely and not painting each person and situation with the same brush. Leaders in these organizations also recognize that poor performance, or so-called bad behavior by an employee, does not mean the person is bad. They understand that behavior is learned. We often are compelled to remind participants in our leadership and coaching programs that no one is born with bad behavior, it is learned. Unfortunately, many organizations have created an environment where poor behavior can flourish. We will get into this in more detail soon.

In old energy organizations there is often an underlying belief that the manager actually has control over the behavior of another person. We set ourselves up for disappointment over and over again by managing from this belief system. Some old energy organizations have created full training programs for leaders on how to manage difficult people. Now consider new energy organizations where there is a belief that if the leader is not getting the results they want, they need to change how they *approach the employee*. The key is to recognize that no employee is *broken* and requires fixing. Trying to fix another person is insane and never works. I know we don't call it fixing or controlling, instead we talk about redirecting or performance management but our actions, conversations, and approach create an energy that often feels very negative and judgmental with an element of fixing. If you look at it from the employee's perspective, that is exactly how it often feels. How your employees *feel* matters and is directly related to their output. Your employees are savvy, smart, and intuitive; they often know what you are thinking and feeling without you ever saying it. They sense your energy. If we lead from a place of fear people will behave from a place of fear. But if we lead from a place of love and compassion people will begin to behave from a place of love. You would probably be surprised how quickly things can change when we change our approach.

New energy organizations naturally lead from a place of love (take another look at Table 2.1 from Chapter 2). There is a belief and understanding that we get significantly better results when we create an environment that includes all of the attributes from the right side of the chart. Just imagine leaders feeling gratitude for what they have, knowing, and more importantly, feeling that the organization has enough resources to accomplish its goals.

What type of energy does a leader emit when they are *feeling* emotions of gratitude, trust, compassion, abundance, joy, and patience? What type of meetings, conversations, and interactions take place when the leader is working with these emotions versus feelings of anger, mistrust, lacking, impatience, and competition? Which emotions will get a better result? Intuitively we know that emotions that stem from a place of love create significantly better energy. We could also note that the emotions that stem from fear (in a business context) reside in the brain and with the ego (thought forms) while the emotions that evolve from a place of love are generated through the heart center (intuition, gut feel). It is important to note that emotions that are positive can also begin as a thought form. In later chapters we will dig deeper into how thought forms create emotions and the resulting neurochemistry and how this impacts decision making and performance. It's all connected and ultimately impacts the energy we put out and the results we get. Leaders in the new energy organizations understand this and practice specific techniques to manage emotional intelligence.

Have you ever walked into a meeting and simply known by the energy in the room that the meeting was going to be difficult and adversarial even though nothing had been said yet? We actually have the ability to feel energy. We will get into this in more detail in subsequent chapters but for now what is important is that new energy organizations completely

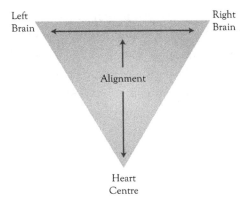

Figure 3.1 Left Brain, Right Brain, Heart-Center

understand this and use it as a meaningful and valuable tool. They know that when they can create an organization grounded in and led by love, they are able to get significantly better results than if the organization is primarily leading from a place of fear. It is important to note that I am not suggesting that we should downplay our left brain, intellectual cognitive knowledge. In fact, it is the opposite. It is simply about balancing our linear brain (left brain), creative brain (right brain), and our newest tool, the heart-center. Including our intuitive innate abilities, also referred to as our spiritual or emotional being, is so important.

Figure 3.1 shows the important balance that is needed in order to feel personal alignment. When a leader or individual works to tap into and balance the right brain, left brain, and heart center, we can create alignment that is powerful and life changing.

Summary

New energy organizations fully understand that the human being is far more than a left and right brain and that when we can engage the full person in a meaningful way, we have the opportunity to create a context for incredible performance, commitment, and creativity. New World Leaders recognize that their primary responsibility is not to manage performance but to create an environment (context) where individuals can and do hold themselves accountable for outcomes and overall performance. Traditional performance management and progressive discipline is the last resort. The leader recognizes they can only create this environment from the inside out. Meaning that they must lead self first and foremost and set an example of consistency, alignment, love, and balance. We will explore all of these concepts in depth as we look at the fundamentals of leadership and then move to higher levels of leadership that include the tools and techniques of The Accountability Model and the core attributes of Spiritually Aligned Leadership®.

CHAPTER 4

Leadership Basics

There is nothing worse than going into a leadership development class sponsored by your employer where the trainer either states or implies that they have knowledge or understanding of how you should best lead. They share the top 10 things all great leaders do and teach to a set of core competencies that someone else developed, someone who may or may not work in your unique environment. The end of the class leaves you feeling inadequate and frustrated at best. More notable are the number of binders on the shelf that are never referenced again or used in a practical and meaningful way.

One of the most important things about leadership development is the understanding that it is different for every single leader. No two leaders are alike. I would never be so arrogant as to suggest that there is only one way to be a great leader, or that all leaders must use the same tools, or stretch in the same areas. Each leader's opportunities are unique. The only exception to this is that love is a common emotion we all share and my experience is that when it's consistently present, everyone wins.

We believe the goal of any leadership development program is to present as much information and practical tools as possible and then create a safe space for the leaders to explore, reflect, and be curious about what *they* may need and want to work on. No one knows you better than you. The only thing we ask of the leaders we work with is that they open their minds to allow new ideas, new energy, and new tools to enter their energy field. When a leader becomes open to exploration and discovery of themselves and their leadership style, there is the opportunity for great shift.

Self-leadership is a natural and organic human attribute that simply needs space to emerge. This in turn has an impact on those around the leader. The greatness of all organizations lies within the greatness of each and every leader and frontline contributor. It is simple: One leader at a time impacts one contributor at a time. Leadership development must come from the *inside out* not from the *outside in*. It is about personal evolution; a true journey. Great leadership is more about a personal philosophy, positive psychology, and a solid understanding of human behavior. We refer to this type of leadership as Spiritually Aligned Leadership because finding truth and alignment is unique for each leader and is based on the personal relationship that leaders have with themselves.

A Note on Process

Leadership transformation requires time. New skills must be internalized and completely owned by the leader for them to have any long-term, sustainable impact. That is why the three and four-day leadership immersions don't work. We end up having the motivational high for a few days and then we relapse into the Monday morning routine. There is no sustainable or transformational shift that resonates from the *inside out*. It is nothing more than a knowledge dump. Real leadership is an ongoing evolution.

If you are hiring a vendor, look for a progressive leadership program that runs for a minimum of nine months to one year with classes that meet half a day, once a month. This provides a touch point every month with the faculty or coach and provides time for the practice of new skills, reading, reflection, and the implementation of experiential exercises. The goal should be to immerse your leaders in an ongoing leadership exploration. Our ability to absorb new skills and ways of thinking and being takes time. The newest research in neuroscience explains why this matters. I cover this topic in Chapter 5.

Leadership programs should also include confidential one-on-one coaching. Leaders need a safe and private space to explore their unique challenges and opportunities. In the New World Leadership programming, we don't report which leaders participate in the confidential coaching, we only report how many coaching sessions we have provided each month. Some still feel that participating in coaching shows weakness and in order to ensure easy, safe, and respectful access, we don't report who is involved. This creates the best environment where leaders will feel safe to access the coaching as needed or desired. This does not mean that there are not some circumstances where mandatory coaching is necessary and required. However, in the context of overall leadership development, coaching needs to be voluntary, where the leader is ready and willing to do the tough work of self-exploration.

Finally, when considering a leadership program, it is critical to look for something or create something that has an ongoing touch point. For example, a monthly tele-class that is open to every graduate. New topics are explored as research becomes available and old topics are revisited. This process allows for a continuous focus on new energy and allows the leader to stay connected. The goal is to immerse leaders in an ongoing conversation, with new ways of being and doing and to create a community of practice.

Stepping Into Our Goo

Leadership gifts reside in the area of challenge and opportunity, not in the area of natural strengths. This is such an important concept. When leaders rely on their strengths without stepping into their true areas of opportunity (the goo), they struggle to evolve. They do not stretch and they stay protected from vulnerability. This will never serve an organization. Leadership is supposed to be prickly. A willingness to be vulnerable is critical.

How many leaders simply go through life on autopilot using the strengths and gifts they naturally have? This is so easy to do and we understand why it happens. It is what we know. However, there is a whole new world out there with new gifts and talents to explore. We sometimes have leaders say, "But my gifts have served me well." Of course they have and we would never suggest that you should stop using them. However, if the only tools you use are the ones you come by naturally, you are limiting yourself and your team. You will see your work and relationships through a very limited lens to the detriment of other opportunities. Becoming open to new ways of doing, being, thinking, and acting is where all the opportunity lies.

This means we must believe in fluid intelligence and not simply a fixed set of attributes. Leaders that believe in fixed intelligence often believe that both themselves and others cannot learn new skills or that they are limited (Caproni 2012, p. 11). For example, they may believe a specific employee is technically weak. This belief impacts how the leader approaches and works with this individual and it soon becomes a self-fulfilling prophecy. The leader assigns the technical work to another individual, never giving the employee in question a chance or the necessary training to learn the required skill. Leaders who believe in fixed intelligence limit their own growth and development, but more importantly they limit that of their team members.

At the age of 48, I decided to go back to university and do my postgraduate degree. I was terrified as I had not been to school for over 20 years and with my personal upbringing and ingrained limiting beliefs about my intellect, I thought I was sure to fail. It took a significant amount of courage to believe that I could do it. Once I changed my attitude about my abilities to learn, huge opportunities and discoveries about myself were made. Research studies in neuroscience explain why this is available to all of us once we make the decision to step into our goo.

Your beliefs about yourself as a leader have a huge impact on your beliefs about other people. Evaluate them and ask yourself, "What do I believe about intellect, learning, and our ability to grow, evolve, and stretch?" Self-exploration is not easy, it takes courage, an open heart, and an open mind. Great leadership does not live in the status quo but in the willingness to view the world, and your role in it, from a new perspective. The truly successful leaders are those who have a belief that they never stop learning about themselves and others and that being open to explore, discover, and stretch into the unknown is truly where high performance resides. In today's ever-changing world this approach is critical.

After decades of research on managerial derailment, researchers have concluded that managers who derail often share similar characteristics. They tend to have limited self-awareness. In particular, they are less likely than successful managers to be aware of their styles, strengths, weaknesses, and biases. Equally important, they tend to be unaware of how they are perceived by others. Furthermore, managers who derail often overestimate their abilities and overrely on strengths that served them well in the past. Consequently, they tend to use a one-size-fits-all approach to solving problems (Caproni 2012, p. 4).

The research indicates that what predicts success is a leader's willingness to stretch themselves, be proactive in their development, and to be

Figure 4.1 Leading self

open to new ideas and to learning new skills (Caproni 2012, p. 12). This applies to leaders at all levels, including senior executives. The leaders' optimism about the world and their team members, combined with emotional intelligence are also predictors of success. Conversely the number one predictor of derailment is relying on the natural skills that helped you obtain your first leadership role to the exclusion of stretching into new areas.

Figure 4.1 depicts the fundamentals of leading self. At the core of every New World Leader is the fundamental belief that leading self is the most important attribute a leader can have, regardless of where they are in their career.

There is a deep understanding that if they focus on their personal leadership, the rest of the leadership responsibilities take care of themselves. They create an organic influence where others simply want to follow and want to learn how to lead themselves toward personal and professional success and 100 percent accountability for results.

Leadership Begins With Self-Awareness

The Harvard Business Review has stated for years that the most important leadership attribute is self-awareness. This belief goes back hundreds and even thousands of years. *Knowing others is wisdom, knowing yourself is Enlightenment* (Lao-tzu and Mitchell 1988). I have personally witnessed the significant impact that occurs when a leader begins to understand how they interact in the world and how others perceive them. It is like the opening of a window for the first time, fresh air suddenly rushes in.

Self-awareness is critical, it is rudimentary, it's a starting place where all growth and evolution begins. True leadership development is understanding the expanded evolution of the person, the connection to their inner truth and alignment, and how they connect this back to their leadership role within the organization. At the highest level of Spiritually Aligned Leadership, self-awareness leads to self-understanding, exploration of impact on others, and the utilization of specific and intentional tools. It is what we do with self-awareness that matters.

Self-awareness can easily be explored through the use of psychometric assessment tools based on Jungian Psychology, Dr. Marston's research on human behavior, Dr. Eduard Spranger's work in the field of motivation and drivers and, in more recent years, emotional intelligence. There are numerous tools that an organization can use. Myers Briggs Typology, DISC, Herman Brain, EQi-2.0, Insights, Pearman Personality, and 360° assessments are all valuable tools and there are many more not mentioned here. A psychometric assessment tool should never be the complete basis of your leadership development strategy but it should be a part of it.

A word of caution: If these tools are used when an organization is not ready for full evolution into the new energy of organizational life they can easily become a way of labeling each other, creating more boxes, and stifling growth and development. We also believe that the tools used should always be the personal property of the person who entered the data. The corporation does not own these tools and resulting reports. They should be seen as a personal opportunity for development and not used as a performance management assessment or in a formal development plan.

If we use the information gleaned from a psychometric assessment to justify in our minds how great we are and how our natural gifts serve the organization, we might simply set ourselves up for a future derailment. This does not mean we don't want to recognize what we do well but if we close ourselves off to new approaches, we become linear and single minded.

I recently had a CEO state, "I would like you to do a full assessment of each of my executive team members and then teach them how to communicate with me." Without realizing it he had instructed me to help him train his team how to interact with him. My sense was that he wanted his life to get easier and wanted people to adapt to his style because it was the right style. There was not discussion on how he might adapt to their styles.

Here is another example. Many years ago I was working with a vice president of operations who led with a very strong extroverted thinking preference or Dominant Style. My client loved a good challenge and drove process and people all the time to achieve results. She viewed herself as successful and if your definition of success is title, money, position, and delivering results, then *yes*, she was successful. She also truly cared about her team and intellectually knew it was important to connect to her team as individuals. However, her style showed up very differently than how she intended. She also did not align well with the guiding principles, organizational culture, and the organization's desire to create high performance in others. Often if an extroverted thinking style is combined with an introverted thinking style (Jungian language) also known as Dominant combined with Compliance Style (DISC language), it can appear as a need for control and a belief that they already have the right answers to most problems. My client viewed her most important role as getting the job done quickly and then moving onto the next challenge. What she failed to consider is how her leadership style manifested itself and the unintended results. This leader actually stated in an open discussion in one of our classes, "All of my direct reports like to be told what to do." Reading the expression on the faces of her colleagues when she said this was very interesting. One of our favorite sayings, that we rely on to create reflection is, "We train people how to treat us." This was a perfect example. The leader, in a position of authority, was training her directors to act and respond in a certain way.

One of this VP's directors stated to me, "I don't really have to prepare for meetings, often the VP does all the talking, tells us what she wants, and we leave without contributing anything to the discussion or decision making." Unconsciously the VP had trained her directors to execute based on what she wanted, and not to contribute new ideas, not to challenge process, or think for themselves. This was not an intentional result but a by-product of her approach. She unintentionally trained people that, life is easier for me when I simply do what I am told. However, if a key part of a leader's role is to develop the next generation of leaders and to model the way to get optimal performance, then this leader is really missing the mark.

When a contributor is not encouraged to provide an opposing viewpoint, they often feel unheard and believe that they are not taken seriously. Contributors feel the energy the leader emits, they feel the vibe. We are going to discuss energy in more detail in Chapter 5.

We have also worked extensively with the opposite situation where a leader has a strong introverted feeling preference or Steadiness Style. This appears as being highly collaborative with a need to include everyone and to seek the views of all contributors. The leader truly wants everyone to feel great about their work and to be included in all decisions. This is wonderful until the leader discovers he or she is using this natural preference to the exclusion of other leadership attributes. For example, this preference can appear as avoiding conflict, seeking harmony, with extensive energy output to ensure that they solve every conflict and challenge in the workplace. They believe this is their responsibility as a leader. They take on the problems and challenges of others, continuously trying to solve team problems instead of encouraging colleagues to resolve their own issues. The story they often tell themselves is, I don't want to hurt anyone's feelings. In many cases the more honest answer is, I really want to avoid conflict. At the core of this situation is a leader protecting him- or herself, not the other way around.

We suggest that you fully understand your natural preferences and leadership style and become highly self-aware of your gifts and liabilities as a leader. Evaluate honestly how much you rely on your natural gifts in day-to-day interactions and do not be afraid to ask yourself the following hard questions:

- Do I sometimes get stuck in my thinking based on my natural preference?
- Do I see the world and our corporate challenges through a limited lens?
- What's my impact on those I lead, what do they say and think when they leave a meeting I have chaired?

- How open am I to viewing challenges and opportunities from a new perspective?
- How open am I to the views of those that are very different from me?
- Am I asking for and receiving feedback from my colleagues and direct reports on a regular basis?

This *is* the starting place. It is a very personal and an internal process where being completely honest with yourself about your blind spots, liabilities, and limiting beliefs begins to open you up to new possibilities, new understanding, and a new view of leadership and corporate life.

What we know to be true is this: Highly effective leaders are aware of their gifts and their liabilities. They do an accurate self-assessment of the overuse of preferences or style and they begin to stretch into the unknown. They accept that leadership development is prickly and that it is not always easy but that the rewards are huge for themselves and those around them. They begin to truly value and appreciate those that are different from them because they are actually willing to step into the leadership arena with an open mind and an open heart. They begin to see the world through multiple lenses and not simply through a linear approach.

We Are More Complicated than Our Preference?

Of course human beings are more complicated than simply the natural preferences or style we were born with. We often use the analogy of a pot of soup. Our natural preference or style is the base of the soup, the way we were born. Then life happens, parents, teachers, and experiences. Your soup continues to have ingredients added to it. A person who loses a parent at a young age will be profoundly different from someone who has not had that experience. A person who was raised in a very trusting environment may be more likely to trust. They may have a lot of trust in their soup. Some of us have a lot of some ingredients and are completely void of other ingredients. Our willingness to do the hard work of identifying what is in our soup and what is not is important. One senior leader stated clearly to me upon our initial meeting to debrief an EQ report, "I don't trust anyone including my own wife so don't expect me to share anything with you." His soup was very different from mine making us very different leaders even though our natural preferences may have been very similar.

Perception

Each individual person sees the world through his or her own unique lens or perception. This is a profound piece of information. Many great scholars and enlightened teachers and religious groups have been teaching this in one form or another for centuries. A simple quote, *We see the world not as it is but as we are* taken from The Talmud, a central text of Rabbinic Judaism written in the 8th century AD, is a clear example of this. The concept of perception and how we see the world through our personal experiences, preferences, and environment holds an important key to leadership in the 21st century.

We live in a world that likes to create scenarios that include winning and losing, good and bad, right and wrong, fair and unfair. This approach has many similarities to the discussion on *love* and *fear* being the two key emotions in the world. It creates silos, divisions of power, and a sense of winners and losers. But when we truly understand perception and its impact, it allows us to create a new paradigm about conflict and debate. It is these simple concepts that make the difference between high performing groups of people and groups in conflict. When you have a team of 15 people there are usually 15 different perceptions of a situation, a decision, or a study. Perception infiltrates everything.

When leaders respect the true diversity within their teams they can have the necessary debate and discussion about the issues. They have positive regard for differences, see the good in their colleagues and are open to viewing the situation from many angles. This is where true appreciation for differences lies. Most importantly, evolved New World Leaders know and accept that their way is only one way of viewing the information and just because it is different from others does not make it wrong or right. There is an understanding that there is no right and wrong in the debate. We can adamantly disagree and both be right, we are right from our own viewpoint and perspective. One of the important roles of hierarchy within the new energy corporation occurs when agreement cannot be met. In this instance someone at a more senior level can break the tie without others feeling wronged. As we work with the accountability model it will become clearer how to integrate this thinking into your everyday interactions. It is of course a long-term practice and not a simple fix.

Effective Communication

Communication is one of the most important topics of all. It shows up in almost every context throughout our organizational life. It doesn't matter what business we are in, communication impacts our ability to be effective. It is a huge topic that often takes up a significant amount of time in most leadership programs. We believe that it is actually much easier than most experts make it out to be. Let's break it down simply and in a concise manner.

Each of us has a natural communication style. It is influenced by our preference or style, upbringing, education, and life experiences. Some of us process very quickly and communicate outwardly like in the case of an *extroverted thinker*. Some of us are verbose and speak loudly, while others are quiet, reflective, and speak slowly. We are all different. Most leaders have a unique style of communication that works perfectly for them. However, the important question is: *Does it work for those you lead?*

Albert Mehrabian, professor Emeritus of Psychology at the UCLA, is best known for his work in communication, the elements of interpretation of communication, and the significance of nonverbal communication. Traditional managers and supervisors in old energy organizations believe that their role is to deliver information to the team, explain what is to be done, what the final expected deliverable is, and how they want things executed. There is less intentional thought given to the *how* to communicate, but there is a lot of thought to *what* should be communicated. This again leads back to other concepts already discussed like *being versus doing, intentional and deliberate leadership versus autopilot.* There is a sense of responsibility on making sure that the correct and accurate message is delivered. We spend very little time considering *how* it should be delivered.

Albert Mehrabian's research has concluded that only a very small percentage of our communication, the *words* we use, impacts the success of delivering a message. In fact, only 7 percent of our communication comes from the literal word. The rest of our communication relies on the interpretation of those we are communicating with (the listener or the other party). The receiver interprets the leader's body language and tone of voice and it is this interpretation that is responsible for about 93 percent of all communication (Mehrabian 1971). So what does this actually mean? It means that as you speak and communicate the other party is evaluating and interpreting everything through their unique lens or perception. *How* you communicate is everything. For example, when you go to Gramma's house on Sunday night for dinner, do you communicate slightly differently than you might on Friday night at the soccer field? It isn't that you will simply use different words but you will actually use different body language, tone, and pace of communication. This is exactly what Albert Mehrabian is referencing. How we communicate is so much more important than the words we choose.

We not only need to consider the unique communication needs of the other person (the listener, contributor, colleague we are communicating with), but we also have to be sensitive to the energy we take into the communication. Am I emanating positive energy that is open and from a place of exploration or am I emanating negative energy or energy that is grounded in compliance and fear? Have I considered the unique communication needs of the other person and adjusted my style to meet that need? This is the leader's responsibility. It seems like a lot of work but in fact with a little practice is not hard. If we want to be successful in building a context where responsible self-management can reside and flourish it is our duty and should be our pleasure.

The leader becomes the facilitator of great communication, flexibility, clear understanding of differences, talents, and attributes within the team. We come back to the statement: *Leadership has everything to do with the leader and nothing to do with the leader at the same time.*

The Importance of Commonalities and Ego Interference

Ego is a topic that senior leadership groups are getting more and more comfortable exploring. We know it is not easy. Our ego plays a huge role in everything that we do. The reason why spiritually aligned leadership attributes are difficult to internalize is that the ego would prefer that we do not. What do I mean by this? Well as you read the sections on self-awareness and communication, you are able to logically relate to the material. It simply makes sense. However, our ego can make applying and practicing these approaches on a daily basis somewhat difficult.

Why is it so difficult to truly internalize (way of being) and access what appears to be so easy and logically sound? This is because we need to be able to truly know and accept that our way of being is only one way of being. On the inside our ego would believe our way of being in the world is the right way. Logically we know this is not true. For every person in the world there is a unique way of interacting in the world, so our ability to recognize this, and most importantly internalize and honor it, is significant.

Although our pot of soup can never be like anyone else's there are some important human commonalities that when understood and utilized can help soften the ego. For example, we need to make meaning in our lives. This includes an opportunity to understand and determine our values, truth, and what is real for us. Our need to ask and answer the question, "Who am I?" (Albert, Ashforth, and Dutton 2000, p. 13; Frankl 1959). We also need to have a sense of belonging and to be appreciated for who we are (Baumeister and Leary 1995, p. 497). As human beings we are basically a social animal that needs a sense of community and interpersonal relationships. A lot has been written about self-efficacy over the years. In simple terms this is the need to feel competent in an area of value to you (Bandura 1986; Paunonen and Hong 2010, p. 339), a common trait of being human. One of the more important needs is the need for control. People, including your employees, need to feel a sense of control over their day. This includes a sense of ownership (Ashforth and Saks 2000, p. 311; Krause and Shaw 2000, p. 617; Bandura 2001, p. 1). Finally, our need for consistency (Feldman and Rafaeli 2002, p. 309; Kelvin 1977) is also important. Most people want to feel that tomorrow will be similar to today and things are orderly and somewhat predictable. This can create conflict within us as we also need to be somewhat adaptable in our changing world. It is a balance. When leaders understand what our commonalities are and use this information in their leadership approach it is very helpful. Focusing on what we have in common can often help us navigate through times where the ego is running the show.

We tend to believe that ego shows up the same for everyone but this is not true. Ego appears differently in different situations with different people. Ego can be as much an internal process as an external action.

For some, the ego is very obvious when it appears externally in body language, tone of voice, and how an opinion is shared. It can appear as an absolute, a belief that the person has the *right* answer. They speak in absolute truths and sometimes with significant assertive energy. Our experience is that often what lies just beneath the surface of this highly assertive energy is a person who struggles internally with his or her own self-worth and confidence. The ego appears as very large and strong in an attempt to mask what is underneath, a sense of being unsure and vulnerable. In fact, the mere idea of showing vulnerability can be a deep concern for some.

Conversely, we see very quiet reflective and inwardly focused individuals who appear on the surface to be humble with a much less apparent ego. However, this is not always true. The ego can appear with excessive internal voices that are judgmental and deprecating of others and self. A lack of worthiness and self-esteem is often at the core. So in the end, whether the ego plays out externally or internally it often covers up a sense of lacking, a sense of not being good enough, and sometimes low self-esteem. Of course, this is a generalization and we know it is not this simple. We believe the underpinning of low self-esteem and internal lack of confidence has developed over hundreds of years due to forced compliance, fear-based parenting and management, and a sense that only a small few should make decisions for the masses. The conditioning we receive when we are young that states we should work really hard, compete, and apply ourselves relentlessly contributes to the over development of the ego.

The simple act of a leader adjusting their communication style to meet the needs of another person is an act of letting go of the ego and allowing a balanced approach to communication come through. This is a very simple example but an important one. The moment we appreciate the importance of meeting our contributor's true human needs we begin to internalize new skills and let go of our own ego.

Creating a Trusting Environment

Trust is a topic that we dedicate a lot of time and energy to when facilitating the New World Leadership™ programming. It is at the core of building high performance. We cannot expect transparency and honesty if we do not have high levels of trust.

Trust is both a cognitive and an emotional process and therefore requires a full exploration in order to build specific strategies to enhance leadership and team trust. The coaching conversation is one tool that works directly to do this. Exploring topics like vulnerability and power and their opposing forces assists leaders in evaluating levels of trust with their contributors. Leaders who struggle with the concept and practice of vulnerability sometimes have lower levels of trust with their team members. We are often accused of beating trust to death in our classes but clients will quickly state, "in a good way."

Trust has been defined as "a willingness to ascribe good intentions to and have confidence in the words and actions of other people" (Cook and Wall 1980, p. 39). All leadership programs should have a clear, definable exploration of trust and all that it brings.

Coaching as a Leader

The coaching conversation is so important. Why? It is what builds trusts, allows us to access the intellect of all contributors, begins to remove the victim mentality, and facilitates the development of both the coach and coachee. Most importantly it is at the core of building a culture of accountability.

Leaders who master the skills of the coaching conversation engage in much more meaningful conversations with others. They are also more likely to stretch their team members thinking and create an environment of responsible self-management. They understand that their primary role is to assist others with development and plan for succession. The coaching conversation is a great tool for doing this.

I dedicate a full section in Part II of this book on coaching as a leader.

Emotional Intelligence

Providing leaders an opportunity to explore how emotions inform their decision making, communication, and critical thinking is key. A leader's personal understanding of how they express and manage emotions, and how those emotions impact their stress helps inform them in a way that can be truly transformational.

Emotional intelligence (EQ) is at the core of our work with leaders. We draw critical connections between emotions and decision making, as well as a leader's well-being and happiness. When looking to develop a leadership initiative, emotional intelligence should be a core component. We don't recommend using an EQ inventory at the very beginning of a leadership initiative. However, we don't wait too long to introduce it either. Sequencing your exploration is very important. Meaning that once the leader begins their personal journey and has a foundation of personal leadership style or preference, emotional intelligence should be introduced. These Level B psychometric assessments must be administered by a qualified person and should be debriefed in a safe and trusting confidential meeting.

Once a foundation of emotional intelligence is created the fun begins as we take a deep dive into what it is to be human in an organizational context and how we can best serve ourselves while creating optimal performance for our corporations.

360° Assessments

The 360° assessments have been controversial over the years. And as with any feedback assessment we want to be careful in their application. Our experience has been that there is significant value when an organization is ready, willing, and has an appetite for making significant cultural shift. We do not recommend using these tools for entry-level leaders unless the organization is highly evolved. However, senior leaders benefit significantly from receiving direct feedback from clients, board members, peers, and direct reports. As noted previously, senior leaders can sometimes be more stuck than junior leaders and as a result the application of a 360° assessment can be highly effective. The key is properly assessing the readiness of an organization when using these tools. Leaders need to want to create a unique development plan that focuses on specific areas identified.

Summary

In order for organizations to move effectively into the future and create the best possible opportunities for culture shift, these fundamentals must be in place before taking a deeper dive. You can see now that leadership development is not a quick event with a couple of workshops but a strategic approach to transformation, expansion, and evolution. Organizations wanting to compete in the future and who are relying on our new energy employees should strongly consider why, where, when, and how they deliver leadership development. They must also address how the senior leaders themselves can step into this new energy in a way that is open, inviting and accessible to all leaders in the corporation. In Chapter 5 we begin to build a bridge between what is fundamental as a starting place and what is critical in today's environment. If we want to shift from our present cultures to an accountability culture where everyone thrives in an environment of responsible self-management, then we need to access all of the information available to us in the leadership field without being afraid to explore what it truly means to be a human being in a corporate community.

CHAPTER 5

Energy Consciousness and the Connections to Individual and Team Performance

As we set a stage for understanding energy and consciousness we need to reflect on why this might be important to our leadership role, our teams, and the performance realized. The key is recognizing that your level of consciousness and the type of thoughts you have can and will impact your ability to be a great leader. We will start with a micro view and then expand our exploration by looking at the big picture relating to energy and consciousness and the impacts it has on organizational life and resulting performance. We will do this by exploring how our individual thoughts impact our individual outcomes, how thoughts are in fact energy, and how this energy permeates our interpersonal relationships. This will include an exploration of the concepts of separation and individuation and compare it to the collective energy that our teams naturally create. It may appear complex on the surface but all of this is a part of a very simple energy system that when understood, practiced, and accessed becomes a game changer, for the individual leader, their team, and the organization overall.

Everything Is Energy

A lot has been written about the importance of understanding how our thoughts impact results. It is important to first understand that everything is energy including our thoughts. So what does this mean? The definition of energy as per the Merriam-Webster dictionary gives us some insight into what this means.

1. Dynamic quality (narrative energy)
   a. The capacity of acting or being active (intellectual energy)
   b. A usually positive spiritual force (energy flowing through all people)
2. Vigorous exertion of power effort (investing time and energy)
   a. A fundamental entity of nature that is transferred between parts of a system in the production of physical change within the system and usually regarded as the capacity for doing work
   b. Usable power (as heat or electricity) also: the resources for producing such power
      The word "energy" comes from the Latin word *energeia* from Greek energeia active, from energos active, from *en* in +ergon work. Some synonyms are: aura, chi, ki, vibe, vibration (*Merriam Webster* 2017).

The field of quantum physics reveals that everything is energy. It applies to our bodies, thoughts, and emotions as well as solid items that might appear to not be energetic. Even a table has atoms and particles that are changing over time. For our purposes we can look at the brain and the heart, which have an electromagnetic energy field that can now be measured. Using sensitive electrostatic detectors and a SQUID (superconducting quantum interference device)-based magnetometer, the Institute of HeartMath™ has been able to measure the electromagnetic energy field produced by the brain which radiates approximately one-and-a-half inches out from a person's skull. In contrast the electromagnetic energy field produced from the heart extends out several feet (McCraty et al. 1998, p. 359). What does this mean? It means that energy is everywhere including energy fields produced by our bodies that radiate outward. The energy exchange between people is very real. This confirms many of the traditional Eastern medicines that use energy exchange between patient and practitioner. It also means that your so-called intuition or gut feel about how a meeting might go, based simply on the way the air in the room *feels* or your sixth sense, may in fact be based on the energy field you are sensing and exchanging with others.

As noted in Chapter 3 we have all entered a room and before anyone has said anything we could feel that things were going to go well and be uplifting, or that they were not. This is due to the energy exchange taking place between individuals and possibly the energy left in the room by the previous occupants. Of course when leaders are running as fast as they can with crazy workloads it is unlikely they will sense any energy at all. What we know for sure is that every leader can learn to become more sensitive to these energies once they make the decision that it is important, and they learn to slow down and make it a priority. Why is sensing energy so important? Is it possible that sensing the energy field of a direct report, prior to a meeting, could be valuable information? Maybe it is as simple as understanding our own energy prior to important meetings and reflecting on how our energy will impact other people and ultimately results.

The thoughts that we have create feelings and our feelings produce emotions and those emotions create outward energy, which impacts our behavior. This energy is felt every time we interact with others at work. Internalizing this process is important to understanding how our energy shows up and why we sometimes get unintended results. We simply haven't done the necessary work to fully understand our internal processing, our beliefs, and resulting emotions on a topic.

We have worked with hundreds of leaders in many different fields. When we explored this concept with a group of engineers in 2013, one leader simply stated, "I am always able to hide my true feelings when I speak with employees." One of her colleagues challenged her thinking and asked further questions about this perception. As we discussed and debated, which is a common practice within our groups, the leader who made the original statement said,

> Let's take a very simple example. I have an employee who cannot make a straight cut accurately and no matter what he does he continually has to redo his work, wasting significant materials. I have the ability to talk with this employee and explain what he is doing wrong. I can do this with no emotion attached, no negative energy. He will never know that I think he sucks at measuring and cutting.

Now, you had to be there to see and *feel* the energy that exuded the moment the managing engineer made this statement. The whole room could *feel it*. It was a great example of how we might want to believe that we can hide our true feelings but the fact is that we don't have to say anything directly for people to pick up on our true intent and true feelings about a situation. This is closely linked to emotional intelligence (EQ). Our awareness of our emotional expression is a key indicator of EQ and has an impact on our interpersonal relationships. As leaders increase their awareness of their own energy they also begin to increase their awareness of others' energy.

This is a huge advantage for leaders. Becoming sensitive to peoples' personal energy is critical if we want to be an effective leader. As many of us know it is often not what a person says that is so important, it is what they don't say. The feelings and emotions that lurk underneath the conversation hold the truth and these feelings emote energy and impact performance. Leaders who understand their own energy first and are able to sense the energy of others can know when and how to ask great coaching questions in order to uncover the real issue.

This philosophy is very much like building self-awareness and using Jungian Psychology to understand our natural preferences. When we begin to understand how important what we think about is, we increase our leadership capacity tenfolds. Everything starts with awareness and a *thought*. Our thoughts are an important form of energy that also produces new forms of energy that show up in the way of feelings and emotions. These factors have been so undervalued within the organizational context and yet we cannot get away from them. So why not learn to understand, embrace them, and use the energy produced through emotions to become the best leader you can.

I want to be clear that this is not about analyzing everyone at work. In fact, it is the opposite. It is about managing our own feelings and emotions and becoming aware of how they create energy that impact you as a leader and those around you.

Figure 5.1 shows a simple relationship between our thoughts and feelings and how behavior and ultimately the outcomes we get are impacted. We will often ask clients: Is there a connection between your thoughts and the outcomes you get? Some leaders agree that there is a connection, others are simply not sure. We then ask: Does what you think about affect how you feel? Does how you feel create emotions? Do the emotions you

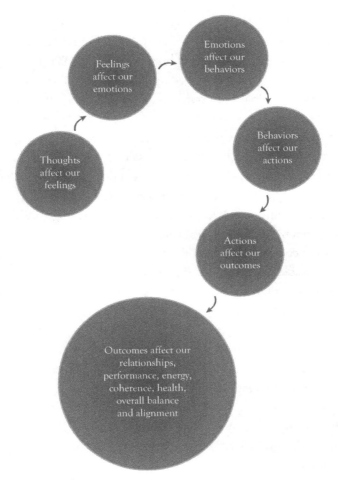

Figure 5.1 Thoughts create outcomes

have affect behavior? Does behavior affect outcomes? I realize that this is a very simple analogy but an effective one in order to assist leaders in understanding that what they think about truly matters.

Old energy organizations focus on doing, creating numerous projects and key initiatives without the important reflection on understanding energy and how this energy impacts end results. For example, a leader attending a team meeting might come prepared to assign tasks and discuss the overall objectives not realizing that the energy they bring to this meeting can have a significant impact on the energy of those attending the meeting. In today's context, the leader's ability to slow down to do this reflection, prior to interactions, is critical to team success as their energy ultimately impacts results. What we know, through the study of quantum physics, is energy can never die, it simply changes form. We also recognize that our old mechanistic way of loading leaders and employees up with as much work as possible, and stretching our human capacity for *doing,* is often the exact reason we get poor results. It is the balance between *being* and *doing* or the delicate balance between intention or desire and surrender that actually produces amazing results. I will explore this further in a subsequent chapter. By intentionally and deliberately managing our thoughts, feelings, and emotions, we manage our energy.

Here is a common example of how this all comes together and why it is so important. Often in organizational life we encourage leaders to support the company position regardless of personal feelings. However, unless the leader has done a lot of personal reflection and their own personal work first, they cannot hide their true emotions and energy emitted. When the leader has not processed their own feelings in a healthy and respectful way, they struggle to deliver the message in an authentic way with the necessary positive energy. Their team members will see right through it or better stated, will *feel* right through it. When a leader does the hard work of asking whether their thoughts, feelings, and emotions are positive and create positive energy or if they are negative and create negative energy, they can make the necessary adjustments prior to interactions. I will provide techniques on how a leader does this and how to work with the tools.

The Science Behind Our Thoughts

The science and medical community used to believe that the brain was static and that new brain cells were not developed past the age of seven or eight years of age. We now know through research, specifically the study of neuroscience, that the brain is constantly changing because of our experiences and the world around us. This is known as neuroplasticity. The common concern about this new discovery is that the average human being's brain is changing without our conscious awareness. This means the brain is creating new brain cells or neurological connections all the time without us being aware. When we have a recurring experience, we create new pathways that wire together to create a new belief system about that experience. If we continue to experience similar things in our lives, we create a story about it and over time it becomes a hard-wired easily accessible neural connection. We find ourselves with long-standing beliefs to the exclusion of new ideas, approaches, and ways of being and leading in the world. The simple term here is we get *stuck*.

One thing I know for sure is that when we can prove something scientifically, we can get the corporate world to listen. Although the field of neuroscience has been around for many years, it is only in recent years that we have begun to apply our understanding into real, quantifiable research with tangible results. When the best in the fields of neuroscience, neurochemistry, psychology, and quantum physics start to collaborate, we are in for a great ride.

The introduction of neuroscience into the realm of leadership is so exciting because we can begin to explore what happens when leaders make conscious and deliberate connections to their experiences and the resulting emotions. Under the direction of Dr. David Rock, The Neuro-Leadership Institute is helping to make these connections through some wonderful research studies (NeuroLeadership Institute 2017).

In our present world of overwhelming stress, anxiety, depression, and endless workdays every leader in every organization needs to have a basic but solid understanding of how our brains (thoughts) impact our chemistry and how our chemistry impacts how we feel, which can impact our decision-making ability and overall focus.

Dr. Richard Davidson is a Harvard graduate and a professor of psychology and psychiatry at the University of Wisconsin-Madison (Center for Healthy Minds-University of Wisconsin-Madison 2017). He is also the founder of the Center for Healthy Minds. He has dedicated his career and research studies to understanding the fundamentals of why some individuals are more resilient and able to flow through life's challenges while others are not. He has studied the brain, neuroscience, neurochemistry, and epigenetics for many years. Dr. Davidson and Dr. Rock are only two of the many scientists dedicating their lives to this important work.

This work is critical in order for us to understand how our thoughts create reoccurring chemical reactions in the body. With recent technology, scientists can measure the neuropathways in the brain (which areas of the brain are firing and with how much energy they generate) and at the same time measure the hormones (neurochemistry/neuropeptides) being produced. With negative, fearful thoughts we create the stress hormones that make us feel anxious, nervous, and on high alert: the fight or flight reaction. If we play the same old story over and over again in our minds, we create the same chemicals over and over. As these thoughts are confirmed by how we feel (hormone creation), we have more of the same thoughts and the cycle continues. From a neurological perspective, the neurons that continue to fire together will eventually *wire together*, making it easier for us to access these thoughts quickly and efficiently. This is known as neuroplasticity. The more we have negative thoughts, the more we create the stress hormones resulting in additional negative thoughts and further neural connection, it is a vicious cycle.

In fact, it is believed that we may be the only species on the planet that can create specific hormones simply through thought alone. Meaning we don't actually have to experience the act of being chased by a criminal to create the associated stress hormones (chemicals). We simply have to think we are being chased or believe we are at risk and we can create the neurological pathways connected to those thoughts. Ingrained beliefs are simply thoughts we keep having over and over again. In a business context, when we create stories or have negative thoughts about our work, boss, coworkers, or employer we create the hormones of feeling vulnerable and fearful of our boss or employer, even if there is nothing to fear. If we have had a bad work experience in the past we may believe we are going to have more bad experiences. We can do this through thought alone.

A simple example is an employee who had a very poor first working experience where their manager treated them poorly and created a dysfunctional environment of very low trust. This employee may believe that all managers are like this and with a few bad experiences this can create a repeating thought: All managers are not trustworthy and will treat me disrespectfully. These repeating thoughts create new neural connections and negative emotions and repeating thoughts can become hard-wired beliefs. As this employee moves into new employment they take those beliefs with them and it impacts their ongoing relationships and possible performance. The new manager is now working with someone who has an ongoing belief about managers. The manager's task is to create an environment where the employee can begin to prune away this belief. However, the awareness of this limiting belief is a critical first step for the employee.

Here is a specific example of how neuroplasticity works. In my early career as an operations manager I worked for many years in the transportation industry. As part of my responsibilities I was required to do a significant amount of travel. Unfortunately, the travel was on a cargo plane in the middle of the night. As a way for the company to save money, managers were required to jump seat on a flight leaving that evening, and then join in on meetings the next morning. Because of my specific role and responsibilities I was required to fly twice a week for a couple of years. During the time that this was required I experienced many situations that I would prefer to forget. Some might think that this is very exciting way to travel; however, when your safety instructions from the pilot are, if I jump out of this window follow me, you can begin to build up a fear. These instructions were common. I experienced many things over that two-year period, some of which were very frightful. As a result, my fear of flying became significant. Although I had previously loved travel and flying I had now developed real anxiety. Just the thought of flying would immediately evoke an emotional response that created a neurochemical reaction in my body producing all the stress hormones including the big one, cortisol. Sweaty hands, agitation, quickness of breath and an overall sense of terror would ensue. Over this two-year period, I had created new neural connections that were clear and definable. Flying is unsafe and I'm going to die. It started to truly impact my life in a negative way.

Long before studying neuroscience or the work of Dr. Davidson I decided to use my mind and personal energy to conquer this fear. I created several practices that helped me prepare for flying including researching the safety of air travel. I created great stories in my mind about the significant skill and intellect of the pilots. I imagined myself arriving safely. Once on board I used a deep meditation practice to slow my heart rate, clear my mind, and remove any thoughts of fear. Within six months I began to feel better and was able to fly with few or no symptoms. Today I fly every week and love it. I have rewired my brain, created new neuroconnections and new neurochemistry. I look forward to flying as often they are my most productive development days, quiet, undisturbed, and relaxed.

Another way that we introduce people to the idea of neuroplasticity and organizations to the idea of transforming culture is to ask them to imagine a dense forest with only one pathway in it. The path is well worn, many people have walked it year after year after year. What if one day you decide you want to create a new path (new culture)? How much effort does it take? What tools are you going to need? Through repeated trips down the new path you begin to create a smooth, easily accessible path but it takes time and a conscious effort. Certainly in the beginning it is easier to take the old well-worn path. As leaders choose the new path consistently others begin to follow and the new path becomes even easier to access. The old well-worn path is no longer traveled and soon becomes overgrown and is less accessible. This is very similar to how neuroplasticity works. With repetition and practice, new pathways get easy to access and old ones more difficult. Now imagine doing that work as a leader, creating a new path in an old energy organization. This is the gift from the field of neuroscience. With a conscious and deliberate approach to our thoughts, feelings, and emotions, we can create new neural connections and prune away old ones that do not serve us.

A close look at neuroscience and the field of positive psychology also contributes to our understanding of how we impact our prefrontal cortex (PFC), where critical decision making is done. "PFC—the most evolved brain region serves our highest-order cognitive abilities. However, it is also the brain region that is most sensitive to the detrimental effects of stress exposure" (Arnsten 2009). When we are in heightened states of stress all of our energy is focused on a perceived threat. As a result, we bypass the prefrontal lobe and are overstimulated by our five senses and rely heavily on what we have always done or known, our go-to habits.

Research was initiated to experimentally manipulate stress levels to see how this altered performance and cognitive abilities. Many of these early studies show that stress exposure impaired the performance of tasks that required complex, flexible thinking, but that it could actually improve the performance of simpler and/or well-rehearsed tasks. We now understand that the type of tasks that were impaired by stress were those that required PFC operations whereas ingrained habit that relies on the basal ganglia circuits were spared or enhanced. (Arnsten 2009)

It is fascinating how much of the new research in this field aligns. For example, Shawn Achor, Harvard graduate, bestselling author and speaker has studied happiness and resilience and their impacts on performance and learning.

Extensive research has found that happiness actually has a very important evolutionary purpose. Instead of narrowing our actions down to fight or flight as negative emotions do, positive ones broaden the amount of possibilities we process, making us more thoughtful, creative, and open to new ideas. (Achor 2010)

Another new important advancement in science is in the field of epigenetics where scientists are studying how our thoughts and the corresponding neurochemicals produced impact the expression of our genes. There is still a lot to learn and discover in this area, but just think of the possibilities. Imagine having the capability of affecting our genes in a positive way through thoughts, feelings, and emotions alone. Dr. Davidson did a live discussion with National Geographic. During part one of the discussion he shares the four main areas of research that support this work: neuroplasticity, epigenetics, mind and body communication, and innate goodness. In the second part he shares his research findings regarding the components that support well-being. The components are resilience, positive outlook, attention, and generosity (National Geographic 2016a; National Geographic 2016b).

So what does this have to do with leadership? Consider the number of thoughts, emotions, and corresponding neuropathways being accessed by leaders each day. Consider the stress many people feel. What if we were able to create new pathways that included positive psychology and positive leadership? What if we created corporate cultures based on abundance, compassion, and love instead of competition and resource guarding? What if we looked at our employees and employers through a positive lens creating positive thoughts and healthy neurochemicals? Would it change the way we physically feel? Would it impact our level of coherence and ability to make great decisions? Could it reduce our stress and hence our corporate medical costs? Could we create new neuroconnections, ones that create more positive hormones and possibly result in less conflict at work? The research suggests that, yes, all of this is possible.

Intuition

How does our intuition play a role in our ability to sense and interpret unspoken information or even events that have not occurred yet? I have worked with many leaders who are in touch with their gut-feel intuition and they will often say they could tell something was going to happen before it did. They may not be able to perceive clear description or details but they get an internal alert to slow down, proceed with caution, and reflect. They might say, "I simply knew that no action was actually the best action and yet I am not sure why."

Intuition is described as a process by which information outside a person's conscious awareness is actually perceived internally by them. This information is often not based on specific, concrete evidence. Or is it? Some scientists are fascinated by intuition and how it works and in more recent years, independent studies have been done on intuition and how intuition impacts our ability to make decisions (The Ideal Changes 2015). There are many unanswered questions. However, compelling research suggests that we all have an intuitive ability and that some people may even have heightened intuitive sense (Murphy Paul 2011). We have all experienced a situation where we enter a room and feel compelled to speak to someone; we are drawn to them with a sense that we have something in common. Conversely, many of us have experienced a sense that we are not going to like someone before they have spoken. Then when they speak we say to ourselves, "I knew it, this doesn't feel right."

There are some scientists that would simply say intuition is nothing more than a person relying on past experiences and through that are able to predict what might happen next. One of the things we know is what we believe to be true is often what holds us back from discovering new things. In early research on this subject, other scientists are uncovering evidence that indicates that people are able to sense things prior to experiencing them, specifically on topics they could not have known or anticipated. We are discovering the true power of the individual human being and my sense is that these discoveries will continue for years to come.

One such study is the work at the HeartMath® Institute (McCraty, Atkinson, and Bradley 2004). The study used a computer that showed random pictures of either heartfelt, warm images such as flowers, children playing, and nature scenes or violent, graphic pictures of accident or war victims. The computer randomly showed these pictures in such a way that even the researchers could not have known which type of picture would display next. The participants were asked to click a mouse and exactly 10 seconds later a picture would appear. Each participant was hooked up to a heart and brainwave monitor. In each case the participant's heart rate would change prior to the negative graphic picture being shown. They could see a consistent change in heart and brain wave action seconds before the graphic pictures were shown. Somehow the participants seemed to know in advance (sense) when a troubling picture was about to appear.

Let's take a different high-level view of quantum physics which may also help to explain intuition. Every life form, including humans, is made up of atoms which contain electrons that move around a nucleus. Atoms communicate with each other using *force carriers or messenger particles* (Shoshany 2014). The *force carrier* is a photon, which uses light waves to transmit information. Scientists are not yet sure how this occurs. The photon is the quantum component of the electromagnetic field. Every person emits bio-photonic energy (Mayburov 2012), which is communicating and sending information to other particles around you. Our magnetic energy field radiates at a certain frequency. Is it possible we are attracted to like energy frequencies and repelled by lower energy frequencies? A fascinating topic that helps us to explain why we *feel* certain things and yet may not have clear evidence to explain them. Communicating through our bio-photonic energy, sending out and receiving information within a constant magnetic energy field, is a powerful communication tool. It helps to explain why we might resonate with one person and not with another, even though we know little about either person.

I suspect there will be many future studies focused on understanding how this innate information system works. However, just being aware that intuition does work opens up our thinking to the possibilities that impact our leadership. Leaders who work to enhance their sensitivity to their intuition may gain greater access to this valuable tool.

Regardless of whether you lean toward the belief that intuition plays a significant role or a minor role in our corporate leadership, most of us have experienced an intuitive sense. We have all had an experience where our intuition, when listened and responded to, has helped us make good decisions and conversely when ignored, we have missed out on opportunities or even made a poor decision. What we know is the expanding research and interest in things that have been unexplored for a century are now taking a spotlight, especially in the context of building great leadership and high-performing organizations. When resources are being reduced and employees, including our leaders, are being asked to do more with less, these innate skills become increasingly important. Why wouldn't we want to tap into every available resource we have as human beings in order to be highly effective?

Can we naturally and intentionally tap into these skills when we are running at break neck speed, busy being busy? Do we want to slow down long enough to tap into these skills? Can we learn the skill of heightening our intuitive abilities by slowing down and becoming more intentional? If so, what are the implications to leadership and organizational performance? Intuition is a powerful tool for leaders especially when coaching and receiving feedback.

Energy Management

Our ability as leaders to create positive energy within ourselves first is the deciding factor as to whether we are able to create positive energy within our environment and teams. As people become more sensitive to energy it is critical that leaders understand what is fueling their present energy. They must be brutally honest with themselves regarding whether that energy is serving them and their organization. If their energy is not serving them they can do the necessary reflection and access the appropriate tools for shifting.

Most of us would say that we want to lead happy, successful, and balanced lives. What we are beginning to understand is that *feeling good* actually impacts the results we get in our personal and professional lives. This may sound like common sense but how many organizations provide time and energy for reflection and energy management? What vibrational frequency do you want to emit when leading a team of people? Most organizations don't have a safe language to have these conversations or the ability to create and develop this skill in their leaders. Negative thinking results in negative feelings which manifests into not feeling well physically. We have a sense of feeling off or out of alignment and even isolated, which over time can cause stress, and in the worst cases, even disease. How a leader feels creates specific energy and can have an enormous impact on how the team will feel. It can also be stated as the *collective energy* or *collective feeling* of the team. This becomes especially important when you are the leader of the team, department, or entire organization responsible for delivering results. Leadership is an inside job meaning that conscious, deliberate internal focus on how we feel, and our energy management are important to our overall leadership effectiveness.

Individual Levels of Consciousness or Awareness

In this section we will look at the different levels of awareness or energy consciousness that each of us can have at any given time.

We all have known employees and some leaders who live in a *victim mentality*. When we ask our clients to describe these individuals they often say they like to blame others or the organization as a whole, they don't seem to take any responsibility for the results they get, they carry a lot of negative energy, which can permeate throughout the department and impact others.

In some organizations the victim mentality is widespread and in others there are only small pockets. However, this level of consciousness is detrimental to all involved, especially the individual living within it. There is a sense of powerlessness and sometimes hopelessness. Is it possible that our old energy organizational structure and culture has unintentionally encouraged the victim mentality? Is it possible that our old energy culture is a great breeding ground for the victim mentality? I believe that old energy organizations, with their rigid rulebooks and policies for everything, create environments where the victim mentality can thrive. The fundamental needs of the human being to have some control and to feel they can contribute openly are denied. Everything the employee does must be within a context set by the organization leaving the employee feeling they have no control, no autonomy and are nothing more than a number.

Imagine the stories these individuals have about their work situation, coworkers, the employer, and boss. They may feel angry, overwhelmed, frustrated, fearful, and hopeless with no control. Their thoughts over time create neural connections and the corresponding neurochemistry. For the manager leading this employee it is frustrating to say the least. For the employee they not only *think* victim but they *feel* victim. Remember that repeated negative thoughts create stress hormones that impact how a person feels physically. It is very real for the person. Having this simple awareness is powerful for leaders creating a different level of understanding. For the leader it is important not to lose faith because by using specific practices and approaches we can assist our team members in shifting from a position of victimhood to one of taking responsibility. They can create new neural connections that will serve them better.

An improved level of awareness or consciousness occurs when the individual begins to take responsibility. They understand that the behaviors and actions they take directly impact the outcomes they get. At this level of awareness, we see people making lists, and setting clear goals and objectives. The person begins to create a to-do list and believes that checking things off will get them closer to their goals. This of course, to some extent, is true. This is where we see many leaders and organizations spend most of their time. They believe that goals, objectives, and lists are critical to business success. This level of awareness is significantly more effective than the victim mentality; however, there are some shortcomings. When we check in with our clients regarding this they will often state that the list never gets finished. As soon as they get close to completing one project or task, several new items have been added. They can easily feel overwhelmed and are at risk of slipping back into the victim state. Fatigue can result when we spend a significant amount of time within the doing level of consciousness.

At a high level of awareness, we see leaders with very different attributes. These leaders are able to work with ease. They create great results with little effort. They are in the flow state, fluid in their actions. They say that the right people and right resources simply show up when they need them. They have plans but no rigid checklists. They believe that when the intention or desire (objective or goal) is clear and purposeful and in alignment with themselves and their organization, the right resources, systems, and people will flow effortlessly. In the book *Flow: The Psychology of Optimal Experience*, Psychologist Mihaly Csikszentmihalyi describes the detailed investigations conducted regarding optimal experience. This research reveals what makes an experience genuinely satisfying and the state of consciousness required. Csikszentmihalyi states, "During flow, people typically experience deep enjoyment, creativity, and a total involvement with life." In the most recent edition, Csikszentmihalyi demonstrates the ways this positive state can be controlled rather than being left to chance. The book teaches the reader that by ordering the information that enters our consciousness, we can discover true happiness and greatly improve the quality of our experiences (Csikszentmihalyi 1990).

There is a calm steadiness to this level of consciousness. We have all had moments in our lives where things just seemed to fall into place, all the right things just showed up at the right time. We can create this state of being in a more consistent way with effort and specific tools, which we will discuss in a subsequent chapter. It is important to recognize that we can change our level of awareness, or specific mentality, by making a clear choice to change our thoughts and the resulting emotions which impacts our internal neurochemistry. For leaders, the only way we can assist our contributors in moving from the *victim mentality* to a higher level of consciousness is to work on our own level of consciousness first. It is helpful for the leader to be one step ahead of their contributors if they want to have the necessary tools, authenticity, credibility, and skill to assist them.

The highest level of awareness is full surrender which is often available to only a very few enlightened gurus. One of my favorite books is *The Surrender Experiment* by Michael Singer (Singer 2015). He shares his lifetime journey of practicing surrender and the amazing results he was able to obtain. The delicate balance of intention or desire and surrender is extremely important in a business context. Too much surrender and we can be at risk of not taking action, waiting for things to miraculously appear. Too much intention or desire can have us pushing boulders and trying to make things happen (old energy). Neither is good. However, when they are in balance and we gently lean in the direction we want to go with alignment and purpose, staying open and curious to new opportunities along the way, we create amazing results.

Separation Versus Individuation

For many decades most of us have felt separate from everyone else. We believe that what we do and think doesn't really impact others. There is a sense that if I do my job, and ensure my assignments are complete, that is all that matters. This is a narrow view often held by old energy organizations. Many businesses believe that if we hold each individual team member accountable for getting their work done it would mean that the whole or collective would be successful. Yes, we may be able to tick all the boxes, but did we get incredible performance? Did we get the *best* people had to offer? Usually what happens is we have several individual tasks getting done in isolation with a sense of separation that doesn't connect energetically. Even if the team has an overall goal or objective and hits the finish line on time, the question is, did they get the best results, the best from each person and the team as a whole?

The more separate a person feels from the whole, the more likely ego will play into decision making and the more individual team members will make decisions in isolation, not understanding and internalizing the energy this separation produces. Often a person feels like a small cog in a very large wheel and they rarely understand the direction the wheel is going. This can increase this sense of isolation and separation. When individual team members feel out of sync with their team, it is impossible to create a high performance. Regardless of whether each team member meets their deliverables or not, there will be a disconnection. So, we are *doing* and are able to tick all the boxes but the actual end product may be less than it could be.

The concept of individuation is different from separation. Individuation is about knowing and believing that you are unique and special and that you will express your gifts and talents in a way that no one else can. Feeling a sense of individuation is very important for leaders and all contributors. So even if you have very similar interests and talents to other team members, no one can or will be able to express them in the exact same way that you do. For example, many of us know an individual who is interested in becoming a professional or life coach. There are many more coaches today than even five years ago. They have a true sense of wanting to help others. They take coaching courses and begin the journey of learning how to be a coach. Each person will bring his or her unique style and approach to coaching. There is never a one-size-fits-all approach in any skill set. We need a variety of approaches in order to meet the unique needs of each individual. A person's understanding and acceptance of their individuation is important to health and well-being. It is all part of building healthy self-awareness, understanding one's true gifts and how they uniquely contribute to the end result.

Healthy individuation is critical to the success of a leader, a team, and an organization. When we take the time to truly care for ourselves and understand our individual nature, we are able to authentically serve others. We must model the way. The problem with the old approach to service as a leader is it can perpetuate the old energy of caring for others at the expense of your personal self-care, your authenticity. It takes courage, strength, and determination to take the road less traveled and commit to self-exploration and self-care. This concept goes against the corporate view of being a team player and putting the organization's needs above our own personal needs. This old energy philosophy doesn't work as it discounts the uniqueness of the individual and completely ignores the fact that how a person feels on the inside is directly connected to the results they get. Understanding the importance of individuation is the only way to build true, positive collective team energy. I do want to add here that this is not about everyone holding hands and being friends. This is about creating a context where everyone holds themselves accountable for the results they get; where everyone is doing the necessary work to become their best with honesty and accurate self-awareness. A leader who is doing their own inner work (leadership is an inside job) is a leader who will have authenticity when they begin to work with their team members. These leaders also understand and honor that each contributor needs space for individuation in order to be part of a highly successful collective.

Individuation and Collective Energy

Balancing our unique individuation while recognizing and honoring our team's collective energy is an important practice. This is a dichotomy which deserves exploration, reflection, and clear articulation. Both are very important and are intrinsically connected. We cannot lose sight of this. Our individual energy impacts the collective energy of our teams.

So what is collective energy? Imagine you are at a concert and your favorite band is about to come out on stage. Sit quietly and imagine this. You know every song. The huge venue is full of strangers, except for the person you came with, and yet you can *feel* the energy, it resonates right through you. People have intentionally invested money and time to be there. They have been looking forward to it for weeks and in anticipation of an amazing couple of hours they are joyful and resonating positive energy. This is collective energy. The positive energy of the people around you impacts you in a positive way with little or no effort, especially if you have been doing your work and are becoming more sensitive to energy. You can feel it.

So now imagine this energy being present within your teams at work. We have seen and experienced this. When every team member is firing on all cylinders and is aligned individually and collectively it creates a positive momentum that is hard to beat. It takes on its own collective energy and is fed by each individual contributor. Collectively the team is moving in the same direction toward a common purpose but each individual is also contributing in an authentic and unique way.

Another example that might help to create the image is to imagine being a part of a large symphony orchestra. You are a very accomplished musician who plays the cello. You were drawn to music your whole life and the cello is simply a part of who you are. When you play it, it transports you to a simple and balanced place, a sense of true alignment. You are in the flow. You know this is what you are meant to do. The orchestra cannot play the amazing piece of music without your talent and unique way of bringing the cello to life (individuation). You know and accept that you are an important part of a much bigger energy. When the entire orchestra begins to play, you are captured in the essence of great music. Your passion for music is enhanced exponentially because the sum is greater than its parts. You are an important part of the collective energy of the orchestra but the orchestra itself takes on its own life, its own energy, extended, collective. It is uniquely different than your personal energy and yet you are connected to it and an important component of it. In the corporate world it helps to reflect on what it is like when everyone is in sync, with great positive energy, aligned to a meaningful compelling purpose. The results are astounding.

What happens when musicians in the orchestra don't really want to be there? They feel out of sync, misaligned and simply showing up for the paycheck. In the eyes of the world and in old energy organizations they can be seen as successful. They have made it. But have they really? This always equates to poor collective energy and a poor end result. Technically they are very capable but their *heart* is not in it and the individual and organization are impacted. This is the difference between good and great.

Here in lies the simple truth, many employees today, especially those in old energy organizations, simply don't have their heart in their work. They are there for all kinds of different reasons but not because it feels great. This is why we see teams and groups of people create less than amazing results. New World Leadership™ starts with the individual leader creating heart-centered work for themselves where leadership, joy, and happiness emanates from the inside out first and foremost. They then use that energy to impact the collective energy of the team. The leader is authentic and able to build a context where others can do the same.

Summary

With all the research regarding intuition, the heart, and its ability to communicate with the brain, we cannot continue to truly believe that the brain is the epicenter of life and decision making. We are beginning to understand the significant impact the brain, in concert with the heart, intuition, and emotions, has on our ability to learn and make decisions. We are also beginning to understand the impacts of our magnetic energy field and the subtle information flow between people.

What is a computer without an Internet connection? I know it seems like a very odd question at this point. The brain is a very good storage device that has the ability to do basic computations. The brain is like a computer without the Internet. It can store a lot of information and can assist us in accessing old information and past experiences that help to inform new decisions. If the brain is all we are using in this day and age, we are missing out on huge opportunities. Just like using a computer with no Internet. Once you begin to include the heart and our intuition, it's like adding the Internet. We are able to scan our outside world, feel the energy, and tap into intuition that feeds us valuable information.

Interestingly, many successful entrepreneurs will say that their intuition is a large part of their business skill set. They tap into how they feel and what their intuition is telling them when making decisions.

The old energy leader believed that success would bring happiness. This belief does not consider that our feelings create energy, either positive or negative. If we are striving for success in hopes of creating happiness but are miserable along the way, it is impossible to create positive results. The old belief of, I will be happy when I have more money, a new job, and bigger house, just does not make sense in light of all of this new information. New energy leaders live by a philosophy that being happy is the first step to creating success. They do the personal work to understand what makes them happy as an individual and then put conscious, deliberate intention toward this. These leaders lean in the direction they want to go. They create positive energy around their desire and intention. When we believe this and practice it, we begin to harness the importance of creating our own happiness as leaders. We become self-reliant, remove any victim mentality, commit to responsible self-management, and know that leading self is first and foremost. This is when the leader begins to have organic influence on others and the ability to create a context where the accountability culture can thrive.

Aligning with a compelling purpose that matters to you, doing work that challenges you intellectually, and feeling that you can be yourself in true heart-centered alignment is a great recipe that creates happiness and therefore success. The energy created by a truly happy person is significantly different than the energy created by someone just going through the motions, working hard to find success. This is a paradigm shift for sure. This is why I often say, the most important relationship you will ever have is the one you have with yourself. It is an individual experience, however, we are never separate or alone.

So why not utilize the innate abilities each human being has, to ensure we are exploring the most well-rounded view of each unique situation. This is a shift that requires us to take a step back from our rulebooks and spreadsheets. It does not mean that we undervalue our evidence-based information, but ignoring those things we cannot see makes no sense either. Old energy leaders might say, "I will believe it when I see it." New energy leaders say, "I will see it when I believe it." They know that there is a clear connection between beliefs, thoughts, and feelings, and the results they get. It is the energy produced by this New World Leader that has an organic, positive influence on those around them and on the collective energy of their teams. This is the new world of leadership. This is how it becomes life changing for the leaders and for all who contribute to the team.

PART II

Creating the Accountability Culture

CHAPTER 6

Introduction to the Accountability Model

There are some fundamental attributes about human behavior that need to be explored in order for leaders to begin to create the environment where accountability can flourish. One of the first paradigm shifts is the consideration that the vast majority of people actually want to be accountable for their actions, results, and success levels, even if they don't know it. Employees don't feel they have enough freedom and flexibility to take action and to use their knowledge to complete tasks. Often they feel that they are being evaluated, observed, and judged regularly, which creates the threat response. This result is not intended by the employer but is in fact often the case. We need to be brutally honest about how the average human being responds to our traditional mechanistic, old energy environment.

We also need to shed the belief that the manager is responsible for the performance of their direct reports. This sets every leader, at every level, up for failure. When we ask leaders if they feel responsible for the performance of their teams, if it becomes personal for them when someone is underperforming or struggling, they usually say "yes." Here is the critical issue. Why would we want a leader to feel responsible for the outcomes of another person? In a subtle way we are removing responsibility from the individual person when we set up systems that state the manager is responsible. Employees subconsciously know that the environment encourages the manager to be responsible for everything and it becomes much easier for them to take the victim role. I myself feel that I have enough responsibility monitoring my own behavior, interactions, and results. Why would I want to be responsible for the actions of another person? Especially when we know it is not possible to control another person.

We say we want everyone to be responsible and accountable for their own actions and outcomes but then we set up systems that don't reflect this. We use terms like performance management and dealing with difficult people (my personal favorite). I once had a human resource manager who asked me to develop a workshop on how to deal with difficult people. I couldn't resist and asked her, "How many employees do you have and how many are difficult?" She stated they had just over 200 employees and most of them were difficult to deal with, in one way or another. I didn't take the work. People are not born with difficult behavior, behavior is learned.

Another example of this contradiction is in the safety world where we say, "Safety is everyone's responsibility." We then create programs, laws, and other systems that leave the responsibility with everyone *but* the frontline employee. We send mixed messages and make it so easy for the employee to simply point a finger and say, "It isn't me, it is someone else's responsibility." These unintentional results are prevalent in many organizations. Leaders telling people they need to be responsible for their actions and outcomes doesn't work but creating the environment where people simply want to be accountable has momentum and power beyond belief. Telling someone something does not make it true for them. Internalizing something, processing it on the inside, and experiencing it, is the only way to make something true for a person.

In general, we create programs and systems that encourage the victim mentality. We unintentionally treat frontline employees as if they are victims of a system that removes their personal power and, therefore over time, they subconsciously begin to act like they are victims of that same system. Remember, "We Train People How to Treat Us!" If we want a different result, we must do things differently. We cannot sit by and tell people to take responsibility when our programs, processes, and management style don't support this.

"Leadership has everything to do with the leader and nothing to do with the leader at the same time." We repeat this several times during our leadership programs because at first it seems like such a contradiction. What it means is that the only way for leaders to create a culture of accountability is for them to do their inner work first and foremost. This in turn creates a different reaction in employees and they themselves begin to shift toward self-leadership. It is a delicate and important balance. Employees are observing, listening, and reflecting upon everything the leadership in their organization does. If managers are doing their important personal work of intentional and deliberate action and emotional management with the right mix of love and compassion (our true nature, freedom to be ourselves), over time employees will respond in the same way, "We train people how to treat us." This process is also very important if the leader is to have credibility and integrity within the team.

The impact of this shift will be felt in every area of the corporation, including recruitment and selection, terminations, self-declaration of wrong fit, and bottom-line results. The present environments that most employees work in are no longer sustainable. However, the moment we begin to tap into what it is to truly be human, including the understanding that people actually want to be strong contributors and be responsible, we begin to see sustainable results. The key is creating the right environment with commitment, longevity, and incredible tenacity.

On Being Stuck

At this point it is probably a good idea to say a few things on *being stuck*. We know that some leaders get very stuck and feel most safe in the old energy environment. They like and use their position and title in order to get results and believe heavily in the old performance management models. These leaders really struggle with the new energy concepts and, in particular, the Accountability Model. This is OK. It is not about shifting every leader but about creating a learning environment where leaders can choose their actions or inactions. What is so amazing about the process is when leaders are exposed to the model and the process, most begin to feel a sense of relief. They seem to intuitively know that this shift can be life changing for all involved. In some cases, leaders can feel a sense of fear of losing control and power and will push back stating that this new way will never work. We have worked with many leaders who were really stuck. We never lose faith as the momentum of this culture shift takes hold quickly with the majority of leaders. Leaders want relief as much as frontline contributors do. People are seeking health, well-being, and an opportunity to contribute in a meaningful way.

As the culture begins to shift, managers, often for the first time in their leadership career, begin to believe that they can bring their true self to work, their more instinctive self, instead of a person who must fit into the old energy box in order to be successful. When we allow our natural humanness to reveal itself, we are able to create amazing results, we have clarity and begin to create alignment.

The Accountability Model

The model shown in Figure 6.1 is the result of 15 years of research, trial and error, and expansive exploration by Change Innovators Inc®. It is critical to state right up front that this is not a silver bullet and will not change your working world overnight. Most of us have a lot of work to do just to wrap our minds and hearts around the concepts. But once the commitment is made to practice, practice, practice you will be on your way to creating an environment where accountability can flourish for your team and organization. The fundamentals of Neuroplasticity are at work. We *can* rewire our brains.

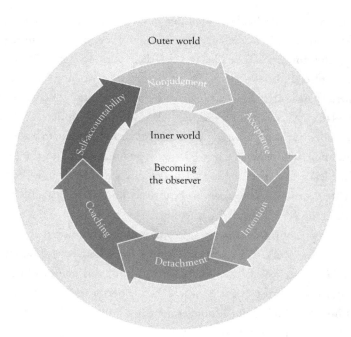

Figure 6.1 The accountability model

Summary

Impacting our outer world requires that we change our inner world first. This means that if we want to create the environment where people can truly become their most authentic self with optimal performance and high accountability levels, we must first do this for ourselves and then pave the way for this to happen for others. As leaders, we must also accept the fact that we cannot do it for another person and that individuals must make the decision for themselves as to the extent they are willing to shift. There are tough questions to be asked like:

> Am I sitting in a victim mentality, am I blaming others, do I feel trapped, am I fulfilled, open and honest? Am I moving toward a solid state of emotional management? Where are my trust levels with my organization and immediate leader? Do I trust myself? Am I in the right role, do I feel a sense of passion and purpose in my work?

These and other great questions will come up as we move through the model, tools, and processes.

The foundation of the model is where our inner world intersects with our outer world. This will always be at the core of New World Leadership and at the center of building a true culture of accountability. In order for leaders to do their inner work I also provide some valuable daily practices that have worked over and over again to assist leaders in becoming more aware of how they impact themselves and others. I hope that you reflect on each of the tools, techniques, and suggested daily practices in order to have the greatest positive impact on yourself as a leader, which in turn will have an organic and magical impact on your team members. As you rewire your brain, you will organically, and with no effort, begin to train those you lead to do the same. It truly is a life-changing experience.

CHAPTER 7

Becoming the Observer

Everything begins with becoming the observer of yourself and the world around you. We cannot become intentional and deliberate in our thoughts, emotions, and actions if we are on autopilot simply reacting to people and life's situations. In this chapter we will discuss the observer from two distinct vantage points. The first centers on becoming the observer of yourself and the second practice involves becoming the observer of the world around you. The first practice fosters your ability to lead from within and awakens your receptivity to your internal guidance, your connection to who you really are. You begin to evaluate how your thoughts and resulting emotions serve you or not. The second practice allows you to evaluate the world around you and the situations and people that impact that world. Both will reap rewards in your leadership role, but more importantly we cannot move forward in our leadership without becoming acutely aware of who we are, what is going on inside of us, and how it impacts both our internal and external world. Figure 7.1 provides the foundation for The Accountability Model.

Becoming the Observer of You

Becoming the observer of yourself means that you begin to observe your thoughts, feelings, emotions, and behaviors, in all areas of your life. It means taking a 35,000-foot view of yourself and monitoring what shows up in your life by asking the following questions: What thoughts am I having right now? How do I feel? What emotions and behaviors are arising as a result of what I am thinking and feeling?

This may seem like an odd concept, but as you monitor the ongoing conversation you have with your roommate, ego, or yourself, depending on how you view your internal dialogue, you can assess its value and contribution to your emotional well-being. Do your thoughts serve you?

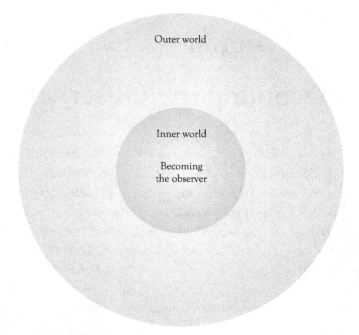

Figure 7.1 Becoming the observer

Do they make you feel good and move you forward in the direction you want to go? Are you creating positive hormones that are serving you well and assisting you in having clarity? If the answer is no, you can make a different choice and change what you are thinking about. If you do not become the observer of you then you cannot monitor these conversations and are no longer able to make a choice. You are on autopilot.

At the center of all successful and joyful leaders is an individual who observes and monitors, in an intentional and deliberate way, what they are thinking about. They observe the subsequent energy they are putting out and the feelings that they create within themselves. They lead from within at every stage of their day.

Sometimes it takes a crisis for a leader to embrace this practice and observe him- or herself in this intentional way. In my coaching practice I have worked with many leaders who are unhappy in their present role. They have negative emotions about their work, interpersonal relation-ships, or the organization in general. The leader is often unaware of how their thought process is affecting the results they are getting. Some simple questions can help them to recognize the importance of becoming the observer. For example, I might ask, "Do you think others around you, your boss, or direct reports know that you are unhappy?" These leaders believe in being very professional and would not verbalize their concerns or unhappiness in an open way, but when asked this specific question they will often reflect on how they show up at work, what their energy feels like. Some of course have been honest with those around them about their unhappiness. I then ask a question around how their unhappiness might affect others and the overall results they are getting. If we want a different result, we have to do something different. That something different is changing what we are thinking about in order to change our feelings, emotions, and chemical reactions. Leaders who begin to practice this get immediate relief.

Personal Evaluation

Doing a personal evaluation often helps leaders to understand where their negative thoughts are and how those thoughts impact their leadership

Table 7.1 Self evaluation workplace

Self-evaluation										
Circle which best describes how you feel in each of these areas of your work life and leadership role											
1 – Needs lots of improvement to 10 – it couldn't be better!											
Duties/tasks										
1	2	3	4	5	6	7	8	9	10
Relationship with direct reports										
1	2	3	4	5	6	7	8	9	10
Relationships with colleagues										
1	2	3	4	5	6	7	8	9	10
Relationship with boss										
1	2	3	4	5	6	7	8	9	10
Relationship with organization										
1	2	3	4	5	6	7	8	9	10

approach. A simple evaluation can assist us in observing the connections between thought, emotions, and outcomes.

In the New World Leadership programming we have leaders complete a very simple personal evaluation. In Table 7.1 you can complete the evaluation for yourself. Consider your working situation, duties, and relationships and score them based on how you presently feel about them. It is important to be brutally honest with yourself whenever you do this type of evaluation.

The next step of the exercise is to examine the area in which you scored yourself the lowest. For example, you may have scored all areas between a 6 and a 10, except for your relationship with your boss where you scored a 3. Take a close look at your results and ask yourself: In the area that I scored myself the lowest, what are my primary thoughts about this aspect of my working world? If you scored yourself a three regarding the relationship you have with your boss, you probably have some pretty negative thoughts that occur throughout your week regarding this relationship. This is a critical observation and acknowledgment for any leader. One of the reasons this matters so much is that our lowest score is impacting all of our other scores. If I scored every area a seven except for the relationship with my boss, it is unlikely I can increase my scores in the other areas to an eight or nine if I don't deal with the area I scored myself the lowest. This is an important part of becoming the observer. Our thoughts impact all areas of our lives if we don't observe, acknowledge, and make different choices.

In one case I had a leader score all areas above a six except for his relationship with his organization. At the end of the class he discussed his results with me and shared that he had relocated from one state to another in order to take a similar role with this new organization. He had family that he wanted to be closer to. He felt strongly that his employer had led him to believe that he would have a lot of autonomy and decision making in this general manager role. The reality was quite different. He was now working for an old energy leader who wanted lots of control and was very reluctant to give any authority to this new general manager. This leader divulged that he had significant anger toward his new organization feeling that he had been misled. This negativity toward the employer was impacting his ability to be a high performer and was probably impacting other areas of work even though he scored himself reasonably high in the other areas.

I was very familiar with the organization he worked with and aware of the very hierarchical nature of the industry. I also acknowledged that the significant size of the organization created some real pockets of old energy even though they were working hard to make the shift. My first question was to ask permission to ask a couple of questions in hopes of building some awareness. Then I asked: What was your previous employer like? Were they fairly hierarchical with lots of old energy? Was it similar in size and scope to your new organization? All to which he replied yes. The industry is heavily regulated and so there is often a lot of fear involved in the culture and although there is some desire to shift, it is a long-term initiative. My next questions went something like this: Why did you think this organization would be any different? Did you get an increase in pay to come to this new organization? Are you enjoying being close to your family? Did you accomplish a lot of what you were hoping to accomplish with your move?

This leader quickly began to have a real shift in thinking. He acknowledged that although the new job is not perfect and there were some things he needs to work on, he did get a fairly good salary increase, was able to buy a nicer home in a smaller community and was now closer to his family. There were lots of reasons to be pleased with his choice. Unfortunately he was focused on the one thing that didn't turn out as he hoped. His thoughts, energy, and emotions were connected to the one area that he was disappointed in instead of acknowledging all of the benefits he received from the move. The risk with this limited way of thinking is that his negative thoughts create negative emotions that will impact his team over time. A great question to ask in these cases is: Do you think your team members know you are disappointed? Even if he is careful not to say anything, it is extremely unlikely that his team members don't feel his energy and ultimately know he is disappointed. His energy can negatively impact his team.

This simple observation of thoughts, emotions, and energy assisted the leader in making a shift that really mattered. In a subsequent class this leader made a point of sharing with me that he appreciated the opportunity to create a new perspective. He realized the first step to improve his relationship with the organization was to begin dealing with his own thoughts, feelings, and emotions. He had become the observer of himself!

Table 7.2 Self-evaluation personal

| Self-evaluation | | | | | | | | | |
Circle which best describes how you feel in each of these areas of your life									
1 – Needs Lots of Improvement to 10 – It Couldn't Be Better!									
Finances									
1	2	3	4	5	6	7	8	9	10
Health									
1	2	3	4	5	6	7	8	9	10
Relationships									
1	2	3	4	5	6	7	8	9	10
Career									
1	2	3	4	5	6	7	8	9	10
Relationship with self									
1	2	3	4	5	6	7	8	9	10

In our open employee group classes, we use another simple evaluation that is equally powerful. These classes are specifically designed to assist employees in understanding how their own personal thoughts impact the results they get in their personal and professional lives. I encourage you to complete this exercise for yourself by completing the evaluation in Table 7.2.

In this exercise participants can evaluate themselves in each of these areas. We ask the same question about their lowest score: In the area that I scored myself the lowest what are my primary thoughts about this aspect of my life? In almost all cases, the participant will acknowledge that in the area they scored themselves the lowest they have very negative thoughts. Here are some simple examples: If a person scored themselves a seven or eight in all areas of their personal life except for finances, where they scored themselves a three, their thoughts about their finances are probably centered around a sense of lack. Some of the thoughts might be, I don't have enough money, I can never pay my bills at the end of each month, everyone else has more than me. The key issues with these thoughts are that they impact how we feel, our emotions, and ultimately our behavior. These negative thoughts also trigger the production of negative stress hormones such as cortisol. The person will generally not feel good when thinking these thoughts. So how do they deal with this? The person will often find himself or herself at the shopping mall on the weekend purchasing something they don't really need in order to make themselves feel better for a very short period of time until the credit card bill arrives.

We can also take an example of someone who scores themselves low in the area of their career. They often have a lot of negative thoughts about their work, employer, or specifically their boss. Their thoughts are often very judgmental with a sense of hopelessness and victimization. The result is often the person overreacts to anything their boss says or does. They don't have a balanced perspective. Their thoughts will create feelings and emotions that will ultimately affect their behavior at work, their decision-making process, and how they embrace other interpersonal relationships. We create, by thought alone, a chemical reaction (negative stress hormones) that can make us feel poorly and result in more negative thoughts. It can become very real for the person, impacting them mentally, emotionally, and physically and most importantly their performance at work.

Let's go back to our general manager in the first example that relocated for a new job. He has found himself with an overcontrolling boss and as long as he has negative thoughts about his new boss, he will continue to have negative emotions creating negative energy between them. He will also risk making poor decisions due to the negative stress hormones that are produced when he feels uncomfortable or under threat around his new boss. Bringing perspective and balance to the situation can only be done if we begin to observe our thoughts, feelings, and resulting emotions.

Sometimes it is easier for a leader to observe how they feel because they get a visceral experience when things are not going well. This can show up as a sore neck, sore stomach, headache, backache, or muscle tension. One of the more obvious reactions is an increased heart rate, but this can sometimes take a while for a leader to connect with and observe. When we have a physical response we can learn to question what we are thinking about and if our thinking is creating negative emotions that impact how we feel physically. When we are running around overwhelmed with work, it is rare that we will notice the physical changes taking place. Many leaders would say they are not even conscious of their physical body, they are only aware of their mind or intellect at work. When we make it a priority to slow down and notice, we can identify the physical shift and make different choices.

This awareness and ownership of the power of our thoughts is an important first step in doing our own inner work. No longer can we blame someone else for how we feel. This does not mean that someone's bad behavior will not affect us. What is important is the recognition that another person's behavior is exactly that ... *their* behavior, not ours. We have choices as to whether we allow it to impact us or not.

Leaders who do this work soon grasp that the situations, relationships, and events that occur outside of them are not the cause of their stress. What causes their stress is how they process the situation, event, or relationship once it enters their thought process. The question is: Do we believe we have control over what we think about and the resulting chemical and physical reaction to those thoughts? Or do we believe that our thoughts are not controllable? Most of us would agree that we have some control over our thoughts. However, we may not know how to go about gaining this control. It all begins with becoming the observer.

Go Slow to Go Fast

One of the most difficult things for leaders to adjust to is the need to slow down in order to observe themselves in this way. When we are running fast and doing, all of the time it is almost impossible to evaluate or even notice how we feel. A leader's ability to slow down and breathe is a very important component of becoming the observer. The breath allows us to connect to our heart, which immediately creates an awareness that allows us to notice things in a completely different way. I will often do a few breathing exercises with the leaders I work with. It is amazing how few leaders actually notice their breath, let alone know how to observe it and use it to assist them. Once they practice it and experience the benefits, they are often shocked at how well they feel, how relaxed they become. They often state the additional clarity in the brain is remarkable. Most highly effective people have daily practices that allow them to connect to themselves in a way that is profound. These individuals recognize the importance of clearly understanding their emotional triggers, challenges, and resulting negative behaviors. The daily practices help them to identify these triggers faster and more effectively. I dedicate an entire chapter to daily practices that we have experimented with for over 15 years and which leaders have confirmed have made a significant difference in their ability to observe and connect to themselves in a profound way.

It Is Not About Ignoring

The process of observing does not mean that we should oppress or push down our emotions. Nothing could be further from the truth. What is important is to observe first, acknowledge, and then ask, why?

This really matters because emotions that are pushed down and ignored will eventually come to the surface and not always in a positive or constructive way. When we do not acknowledge our emotions, choosing to ignore them, we begin to pretend that everything is OK. We go along to get along even though we may strongly disagree with something. In old energy organizations this has been prevalent for decades, which has resulted in high stress levels, mental health issues, and other performance challenges we see today. Suppressing emotions is not a healthy response and will only serve to create larger problems in the future. Take our general manager who relocated for a new job, if he had not acknowledged his anger and frustration and asked himself the hard questions, he would still be going to work harboring these feelings and all they encompass. His ability to observe, be honest, and be vulnerable enough to ask a coach about it, allowed him to process his emotions. He was able to reflect and ask himself the hard questions about the relocation, benefits, and weakness, all of which allowed him to release his anger and realize that he benefited overall in the move. In fact, this leader had a level of gratitude for all that he had gained in the move, which did not exist prior to his important observation and evaluation. Another simple observation that is subtle yet so important is that this leader chose to make the move. He made the grown up decision to make a large move based on his own needs. He could easily have blamed his employer and lived in a victim mentality for months and years instead of owning his role in the decision. Clear accountability is emerging.

Acknowledging how we feel and the thoughts and emotions that are associated with what we are dealing with is very important and a critical part of being the observer. This is where honesty with ourselves plays such an important role.

Disliking Something in Another Person

Consider this statement. *You cannot dislike something in another person that you do not dislike in yourself.* I am not sure where this saying comes from but I have used it for years in our leadership development programming. This is a very tough statement that requires significant reflection for leaders. However, my experience is that when contemplated and evaluated, leaders will agree with its accuracy. For this to happen leaders must be good observers of themselves. These leaders are self-aware and willing to step into something that is often uncomfortable. (Remember how we talked about Stepping into Your Goo in Chapter 4.)

Reflecting on those other team members or employees who you dislike or *push* your buttons is so important when applying these tools and techniques. My favorite examples involve a female leader I worked with several years ago in a group leadership program. She stood up and said that she disagreed with the statement and that it didn't make any sense to her. I knew this leader fairly well and asked permission if we could pursue this discussion in class. She agreed. I asked her to give me an example of something that bugs her in other people. In her mid-50s and with lots of life experience she shared what I thought was an odd pet peeve.

She stated,

I really hate it when these younger employees or anyone dress really weird, out of style, and out of context. For example, they come to an interview completely inappropriately dressed. I dislike it when young people wear a ball cap backwards or pants belted really low, those kind of things.

This person was a highly effective, strongly intuitive, and reasonably self-aware, well-educated leader and I only had to ask a couple of questions in order to assist her in a deep reflection. I asked, "Do you think it is possible that you might be somewhat biased when doing interviews? Does this strongly held dislike impact your evaluation of people?"

Her honest response surprised some of the group, "Absolutely, I would like to think that I can overlook it when interacting with people but I know I don't."

"So think back to when you were a young girl. Were you a really unique individual? Did you dress differently to show a unique style? Did you naturally stand out from others?"

The look on her face said it all. She simply said, "Yes, absolutely."

Knowing this particular leader, my suspicion was that she was ridiculed and possibly even bullied for being different and over time decided to give up her uniqueness in order to conform and be, in the eyes of society, more successful. She subconsciously learned to dislike this about herself as she felt a disservice by it. What I found most interesting was her uniqueness, it was one of her greatest gifts but as with all gifts can be a liability in the extended form. Learning to use that uniqueness in an effective way was so important to her overall success.

You might be wondering why this conversation was important in a leadership class. It was important because her unintended bias was impacting her ability to be fair in hiring and in other interpersonal relationships. She sometimes judged a person by their appearance instead of seeking their true gifts and talents. She might not listen as actively to a colleague's opinion if she deemed them disrespectful in their attire.

It takes courage to step into one's goo, to get honest about the things we try to avoid knowing about ourselves. But it's only when we become aware of something that we have the ability to make the shift. It is easy and almost organic once we recognize it for exactly what it is. The leader in the example didn't want to be like this, but she simply said to herself for years: "It is just the way I am, it is simply my thing." By internalizing this new realization, she could begin to forgive herself and hence be easier on others. She also was able to recognize that one of her gifts is the ability to see things from different viewpoints; she had a unique way of seeing the world. This allowed her to honor that part of her, in a new way, opening up the opportunity to see the uniqueness in others in a positive way.

Becoming the Observer of the World Around You

Imagine a massive auditorium, with the largest stage you can visualize. There are over seven billion customized chairs in the audience. Each person on the planet has a chair that is perfectly suited for them, their body, weight, and height. Your chair is perfectly suited just for you and no one else is allowed to sit in your chair.

The stage is where all of the interactions in life take place, all events, situations, and interpersonal interactions for both your personal and professional life. The purpose of visualizing the stage is to understand that we always have a choice whether we step onto the stage and interact or remain in our seats. Observing the unfolding of life as if it were a stage allows us to make intentional and deliberate choices as to when, where, and how we interact on the stage.   Each one of us is paid for our experience, education, and overall knowledge. If there is something going on that impacts your area of responsibility or expertise, it simply makes sense that you would step onto the stage and interact with others and share your opinion. The question is when do you step off the stage? How many times do you step back onto the stage to restate your opinion?

It is also important to note that there are people who love the drama of life and live on the stage all of the time. They often like to have others join them on the stage. This is why it is important that leaders make choices based on value and desired results. I will expand on this further, in a later section, however our ability to determine, at any given time, whether we want to be *in the world* or *of the world* matters. Being *in the world* means you are observing in a reflective way, making deliberate choices. Being *of the world* means you are a part of it, interacting either consciously or not. It is however a choice, one that you can be aware of by observing or not.

In any corporation there is a unique stage where the daily interactions take place. It is important for leaders to consider how often they get involved in things that aren't really theirs. How often do we have an opinion on something and when we step back and really think about it, we realize it has little or no impact on us? Leaders can also find themselves being influenced by others to get involved in something that is not theirs, especially when it comes to negative energy and negative emotions. People want company so that they can be validated. However, you can never assist a person who is negative by getting into their negativity with them. The only way to truly assist another person is to stay in positive, optimistic high energy, asking great questions and allowing for reflection. Leaders can easily be drawn into sweating the small stuff, engaged in decision making that has little or no impact on them or their team. Everyone has and wants an opinion, however this is usually where ego gets in the way and we end up on the stage trying to influence everyone around us. When we focus on what directly impacts us and do not allow ourselves to be drawn into the drama of someone else's goo, we remain clear and focused on what actually matters. You are responsible and accountable for you, and no one else.

Summary

As you practice the skills of becoming the observer of you, you will soon find yourself observing in a proactive and intentional way. You can then catch yourself when you don't feel right, when you feel off balance or when your emotions seem less than positive. You might then ask yourself: Why am I feeling like this? Why does this not feel right? Why have I been triggered and become emotional about this? Triggers usually mean that someone has held up a mirror for us, an opportunity to reflect. The mirror gives us the opportunity to evaluate the information in an honest way or ignore it. This is a fabulous process for growth and self-awareness, as you monitor how you feel you can intercept the feeling before it manifests as a behavior. Maybe you are having a negative thought about another person or a situation at work. You might be having a negative inner dialogue with your roommate or ego. Catch yourself and ask: How does this conversation I am having with my ego, about this person or this situation, serve me? Note that I have not mentioned observing others. It is not your job! Your job is to lead yourself and allow others to do the same. Focus on your thoughts, feelings, and emotions and not on that of any one else.

At some point in every leader's career, they deal with unwanted and undesired events, personality conflicts, and poor interpersonal relationships. The challenges we face are life's most effective teachers and it is through the difficult times that we show our true leadership capabilities. Having strong emotional awareness is fundamental to great leadership.

Change does not occur simply because the leader becomes a positive thinker. Affirmations or simple positive thinking don't work when used on their own. It is at the emotional stage that real change occurs. *I must change how I feel about a situation in order to impact the outcomes I get.* Emotions are tightly linked to thoughts but change does not occur through thought alone, we must invoke positive emotions. In the section on daily practices you will have an opportunity to reflect on how you can create the best environment for you to monitor your thoughts and resulting emotions. Remember the science explored in Chapter 6. We are a species who can change our emotions and the resulting biochemical reactions through thought alone. Using powerful questions and imagination, combined with positive regard for others and ourselves, is important. The key is to understand how closely linked thoughts and emotions are. When you change your perspective (thoughts), you can change your emotions. However, it does require daily practice. The only thing you have control of is yourself, so make a commitment to lead yourself everyday in an intentional and deliberate way and leave others to do the same. Make a commitment to feel good about yourself and your contribution. Model the way and set the example.

Recognize that the relationship you have with yourself is the most important relationship and that this is where your focus must be if you are to become the best you can be, connected to your true nature. Before you know it, you will be monitoring your thoughts on a regular basis and catching yourself long before negative feelings, emotions, or derailed behavior can manifest. You will have become the observer. It is not hard to learn how to do, but it does take commitment and resolve in knowing that you absolutely have control over what you think about and your resulting feelings and emotions.

CHAPTER 8

Nonjudgment and Acceptance

As we learn to observe our thoughts, feelings and emotions, and the subsequent internal physical responses, we begin to see what makes us feel good and what does not, what creates positive energy and what does not. Now let's look at how judgments impact how we interact with others in certain situations.

Figure 8.1 depicts the next stage in building an environment where accountability can flourish. It is all about you, the leader, leading yourself. It is not about the employee. Our efforts ultimately impact the overall environment and all contributors.

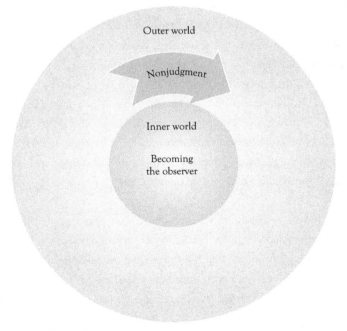

Outer world

Nonjudgment

Inner world

Becoming
the observer

Figure 8.1 Nonjudgment

Let's take an example. Imagine one of your employees is struggling. This person may be the one who consistently underperforms. They may have attendance issues, challenges in decision making, or simply struggle with the work itself. Whatever the issues are, take a moment and think about that one person that consistently creates challenges for your department or business unit. Now ask yourself: What is the story I have in my head about this person and how does it make me feel when I think about this person? We like to think that we don't have any negative feelings in these situations, but if you really take time to be honest and sit with your prevailing thoughts about this person, you will notice some subtle changes in your energy. The thoughts you have and the feelings and emotions that result will impact how you interact with that person. When you need to speak with them about a concern, your energy will usually change without you even knowing it. Now ask yourself: Does the other person know or at least sense that I have these thoughts, feelings, and resulting emotions and that it impacts my energy when dealing with them? The answer is always, yes. A leader's ongoing frustration with a team member who is struggling only serves to make the situation worse.

Take a quiet moment now and ask yourself some different questions. How well do the people I work with truly know the *real me* on the inside? How well do I think my colleagues truly *know me?* Most leaders will say, "They don't really know me at all, they know the person they see at work each day, and they know some things about me, but not the true me on the inside." It is impossible for people that you work with to truly know your fears, worries, concerns, your personal issues, and your past, all of which affect you as a person. This can include your upbringing, religion, traditions, culture, and relationship with parents, siblings, and community, anything that is in your pot of soup that makes up the totality of you.

Each person is deeply impacted by his or her past and present and so the assumption that we understand another person wholly is ludicrous. In fact, many people will say that they are reluctant to share their intimate thoughts and feelings with even their life partner let alone people at work. This is because we are either trying not to hurt others' feelings or we are trying to hide our own true feelings. We are often scared of the value judgments, stereotyping, and isolation that comes from exposing our true underbelly. At work we will share our ego-based work opinions, and hold back and hide many of our truths in order to protect others and ourselves.

I am not judging this as right or wrong, I am simply saying it is the culture in which most organizations operate. Society has trained us to believe it is the best way to conduct ourselves in order to fit in.

Leaders who are willing to step into their goo and begin to truly lead themselves from the inside out soon come to realize that our personalities, carved out over years of experiences both good and bad, are impacting our experiences every day. Hiding them and pushing them down has an unintended impact on everyone involved. Behavior comes from a real place. Here is why this is important.

First, you do not know your employees. You know so little about them, what makes them tick, how they think, and why they are the way they are. As you noted for yourself, people you work with know so little about the real you. So why do leaders think they know their employees? Leaders often label and judge employees based on so little information. We categorize and fit employees into different boxes. When we do this, the energy we bring to working with them is profoundly impacted by the story we tell ourselves about them.

It's easy to label the employees who challenge us as having bad behavior. No one is born with bad behavior, none of your employees were born saying, "When I grow up I am going to torment my boss and make his or her life miserable." However, I know many leaders who have either all, or part of this story, about one or more of their employees. Leaders who are not aware of their thinking develop these stories over time, and allow them to significantly impact how they interact with these employees.

Employees who are struggling have a story of their own that impacts what they do, say, and how they show up at work. In an accountability culture, your goal is to get great performance from each and every employee and to deliver results to your organization. Internalizing that your employees are not numbers, machines, or robots but that they are human beings is so important. You do this by acknowledging their diverse stories and complicated pots of soup.

Does this mean that every leader must become a counselor or therapist in order to be a great leader? Of course not. I would never suggest that, and in fact we never want to take that role, it would simply be inappropriate.

However, we must use our own human capacity, emotional intelligence, and empathy in order to learn, explore, and create a safe and trusting environment where employees can explore their own behavior and build a foundation for personal accountability.

I don't want to get ahead of myself here. At this point the goal is to understand that our strong judgments and opinions about our employees have a direct impact on the results we get. Often leaders are unaware of how they are contributing to the problem through their own energy, and how they show up when working with employees. Unfortunately, we rarely teach leaders the importance of nonjudgment. In fact, it is so foreign to us that it is hard to comprehend. Some leaders, at this point, might be thinking, this is my job to judge my employees and I am responsible for holding them accountable. This belief is exactly the belief that creates the victim mentality. The employee quickly senses that the leader is judging them and taking the responsibility for what is going on. The employee is happy (subconsciously) to leave the responsibility for accountability with their boss. A manager cannot hold an employee accountable for results. This belief simply goes against what it is to be human. The manager with old energy can use the old carrot-and-stick method in order to invoke fear in hopes of the person taking responsibility but we know how well that works. In Daniel Pink's book, *Drive*, he lists the seven deadly flaws of carrots and sticks and clearly notes it does not work (Pink 2009). At best, it has very limited short-term results.

Empathy and Vulnerability

Empathy is a critical skill for leaders. In order to have empathy, we must be able to invoke an experience within ourselves that is close to what the other person is feeling. We must be able to be vulnerable ourselves. It is not about minimizing the other person's pain but simply being able to be with it. We need to acknowledge that we can never know what it is truly like to be another person and that we will never have all of the information in order to feel what they feel. However, our ability to connect with another person relies on our ability to have empathy and to be vulnerable ourselves. Empathy and vulnerability allow us to begin to be authentic at work and this is often what an employee needs to see in order to open up and share what is going on for them. When this happens, our role is never to give advice or to tell but to simply be present and truly listen and ask questions that allow the other person to determine what they want to do next.

Some of our old beliefs like, *never let them see you sweat* are the actual things that hold us back from truly connecting to our team members. Many leaders we work with struggle with the idea of being vulnerable at work. They believe their job is to show confidence, no matter what. However, if we come back to the notion that everything is energy, when a leader pretends they have all of the answers or that they have control of everything, the employee will actually feel the imbalance and know something isn't right. The leader's credibility is now at stake. When a leader can share their vulnerability, be open and honest about what they know and what they don't know, they become human in the eyes of the employee. When leaders share stories with employees that are relevant to the issue, where things did not go so well for the leader, it allows the employee to see the leader in a different light. This is the beginning of authentic trusting relationship.

The Three Hats: Human, Leader, Manager

We like to encourage leaders to consider the three hats of being in a position of authority at work. The hat we believe is most powerful is the *human being hat*. However, all of the hats play a necessary role.

The leader wearing the human hat connects to employees as human being first and learns intimately how to stand in their shoes and create the necessary conversations that can change the dynamics. The leader recognizes and understands their own vulnerability, has high emotional intelligence, and uses empathy as a way of creating a safe environment for employees to be themselves. This practice invites the employee to drop their guard and be their authentic self at work. Remember that we train people how to treat us. If we want employees to be open and honest with us about what is truly going on for them at work, we must be willing to demonstrate this skill ourselves. The human hat is about love, compassion, humility, and caring. It is about accepting that you will never fully understand what is going on for the employee. It is about letting go of your judgments in order to see and feel the real situation. This prepares the leader to ask the right questions.

The *leader hat* can now come into play where we ask great questions and listen intently to the answers. We are open to the views of others but want to move the conversation into the realm of further exploration and discovery. It is an energy that seeks to understand instead of an energy that seeks to be understood. It is a willingness to see problems, situations, and conflicts from all perspectives. This is where the real magic can begin to take place. We can engage in meaningful conversations that allow the other person to be reflective.

We use our management skills in many different ways. We manage process and procedures but lead people. The use of the *manager hat* is certainly an ongoing practice in the running of our businesses but in the context of creating the accountability culture and when working with people, the manager hat should be used very sparingly. The manager hat comes into play only when the leader has used all of the tools and techniques of the Accountability Model consistently but the employee has chosen to remain stuck and unwilling to shift. This is where our traditional performance management practices and progressive discipline tools should be used. There are situations when we have no choice but to use the old mechanistic systems to transition individuals who are so stuck that a shift toward the new culture is not possible. There are times when a person requires a more major event in order to get unstuck. This is one of those times.

When you put on the human and leader hat, you shift the power from the leader's side of the desk to the employee's side of the desk which leaves the employee with specific choices that only they can make. This is done using all of the tools and techniques in the model but it all begins with a willingness to wear the human hat.

Judgment Versus Evaluation

One of the interesting discussions we have with leaders focuses on the difference between judgment and evaluation. Some quickly respond and say it is all about semantics. But is it really? When was the last time you judged someone or something? Most people will say 15 seconds ago. We have been trained from a very young age to judge everything. Parents, teachers, and other well-meaning people teach youngsters there is right and there is wrong. Many cultures are riddled with biases, rules, judgments about everything from looks, money, the car a person drives, not to mention the big ones like religion, ethnicity, and so on. It is no wonder that when we enter the working world we will have a long list of biases and beliefs about right and wrong. We will also encounter employees and bosses with their own biases and beliefs. We will agree with some of them and not with others.

Here are some important questions for leaders to reflect on. How does it feel when you think you are being judged? Does the average person like being judged? What emotions are associated with the feelings of being judged? Are they positive or negative? Do you think that our traditional performance management tools create an environment where a person would feel judged? If we know that we ourselves don't like being judged, why do we create systems that have an overarching process that includes the judgment of others, intended or otherwise?

So, what is the difference between evaluation and judgment? Most leaders will say that evaluation is more objective, it is about an observation, a fact about something specific. One of the key components of an evaluation is that there is no negative emotion attached to it. Let's look at a simple example, a person being late three times. Evaluation is a simple observation by the leader with no negative emotion attached to it. The leader is able to observe it objectively and follow up with no negative emotion versus the manager who immediately goes to the impact of the lateness and internalizes it with negative emotion and deals with it from this energy level.

Practicing nonjudgment is very difficult because, as mentioned before, we are conditioned to judge everything. But remember, you never have all of the information. A leader's ability to recognize that they have limited information, at best, is so important, so is the recognition of the story they are telling themselves about a person or situation. When you acknowledge that you don't have all of the information, you are immediately more open to options. You will be able to address the situation from an objective, nonemotional perspective. Again, emotions are energy in motion and so we must understand the impact the leader's emotions can have on interactions. Ask the question: Is it their issue or mine? Is this something I need to be emotional about? How will it serve me? What will happen if I get attached to this emotionally?

When an employee senses their leader is emotional about something they have done, the employee immediately feels that their leader has an issue with it. The employee may not have an issue with the circumstances. In fact because they chose their behavior or action, we can assume the employee doesn't have an issue with it. Unintentionally it becomes the leader's issue, not the employee's. They are attached to a certain belief and have a certain judgment, which unintentionally makes the issue that of the leader and not of the employee.

Acceptance

I have included the tool of acceptance in the same chapter as nonjudgment because they are so closely linked. When we stop judging everything and everyone, we can begin to accept. The ego plays a significant role when we don't want to accept things, situations, and people the way they are. It does not mean that we don't share our opinion on things, it simply means we don't push boulders. Visualize a small ant pushing a large boulder up a huge hill. I will ask leaders if they have ever felt like the ant. I think that most of us have experienced that feeling of being overwhelmed when we are trying to change something that just doesn't seem to want to budge. Figure 8.2 depicts the next tool and technique in the accountability model: accepting situations and people as they are

Unfortunately, we still live in a society that teaches us from a young age that if we want something, we have to work hard for it and that anything worth having is worth working for. This belief can create an environment where a person fixates on what they desire and then works relentlessly to get it. But what happens when life is not cooperating, when things just don't seem to be lining up, or when someone is not doing what we think they should? We try to change the situation, we employ new tactics in pursuit of our goal, we try to influence another person to see things the way we see them. When they don't, we lament that things would be easier if we all just agreed. We keep pushing the boulder until we are exhausted and sometimes the boulder rolls right over us. If we

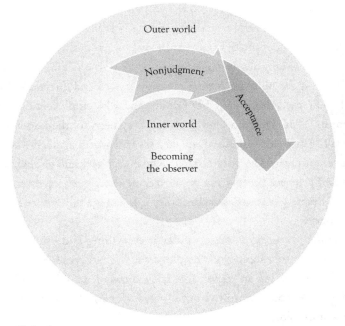

Figure 8.2 Acceptance

are aware, we stop trying to change things but many of us stubbornly return to pushing the boulder again and again. Eventually we end up so exhausted that we give up in frustration.

For example, when we are dealing with employee behavior that is unwanted, we often push the boulder by having multiple old energy conversations, telling the person our expectations and that we expect them to make a change in their approach. The person feels judged and the leader rarely gets to the bottom of the real issue. There is usually negative emotion connected to these conversations and the employee feels it. The employee will often tell the manager exactly what they want to hear and the behavior will improve for about two weeks. Then it goes right back to where it was before and sometimes worse. I think many of us have experienced this. Why does this happen?

The reason this occurs is that there has been no internal change for the employee. Everything was external. It was the manager telling the employee the expectations once again. The manager does almost all of the talking and the employee does the listening. The manager's reaction is clearly visible to the employee. The employee has experienced this discussion before and knows exactly where it is heading. They have learned to nod and say all of the right things. In extreme cases, the employee feels invisible and simply allows the leader to do all of the talking and to take all of the responsibility for setting the expectations and direction. This is exactly how the victim mentality prevails and why employees don't take responsibility. It is because they don't feel they need to, the leader is taking it all. Employees are often not honest with their managers because we have not created an environment where they feel safe enough to do so. When a leader accepts the employee for exactly where they are at, with no negative emotion attached, they can change the conversation in a profound way.

A leader who learns to stop judging everything and everyone, and who begins to truly accept their employees as they are, is a leader who can build the foundation to responsible self-management. I appreciate that this might feel counterintuitive but if you stick with the process you will see how it unfolds.

We are often challenged on these concepts with comments like, "How would anything change in the world if we simply accepted things as they are? What about people who have been really instrumental in making great change, like Nelson Mandela?" Indeed, difficult questions. It is the energy associated with a specific situation that makes the difference. When we are ego driven and needing to change something or someone, we push hard, trying to change the situation. If nothing changes, we often end up feeling frustrated and angry. This upwelling of negative emotion is how you know you are boulder pushing. This in turn creates the fatigue and unrest. We usually don't make good decisions in these situations.

But when a person has positive emotions and positive passion toward a situation, they can let go and accept where things are at, and they find other ways to gain momentum. They recognize that going slow is often best and they can remove themselves from the hill. Labors of love or labors of true passion do not feel like boulder pushing. These desires usually initiate from the heart center, not from an egocentric place or the left brain.

It is also important to note that acceptance does not mean agreement. Just because a person accepts things as they are does not mean they agree with it. It simply means that they choose to view things as they are with no negative emotion attached. They do this in order to create positive momentum, moving forward in whatever direction they choose.

This approach is good for everyone, especially when dealing with conflict or poor performance. The leader releases negative emotions around the situation or person and the employee gets needed space to begin to reflect. At minimum the employee will feel the change in energy. They may even wonder what is going on and why things have changed. This is a good thing.

Summary

For those who struggle with these concepts here are some questions to ponder:

- Does the old way of telling employees what to do and what is expected really work?
- Are you getting long-term, sustainable changes in the other person's behavior or results?
- If you have to move to progressive discipline, are you getting long-term change through discipline?

The goal is to always get optimal performance from each and every person based on their capabilities and skill set and to know when to assist a person to move into a new opportunity. As leaders bring in the tools of nonjudgment and acceptance, they model the way for their employees. Leaders often experience a sense of relief as they let go of all of the negative emotions associated with feeling they are responsible for fixing individual performance. They can begin to accept their team contributors for exactly where they are at and move forward from a neutral place. This is the beginning of creating an environment where accountability can flourish.

CHAPTER 9

Intention

This fascinating topic can sometimes be a bit of a puzzle to unravel and for this reason I have dedicated a chapter to it. Although not a large chapter, it requires a thorough review and reflection in order for a leader to truly understand the significance of monitoring intentions. I also touch on the topic of empathy and forgiveness as it is connected to how we monitor intention. Figure 9.1 below depicts the next tool in The Accountability Model: The practice of monitoring intention. I will provide a few examples that are related to the work environment, but also some that are not, in order to create an opportunity for a full exploration. Exploring these techniques through the lens of our personal lives assists us in fully understanding their impact and importance in our corporate lives.

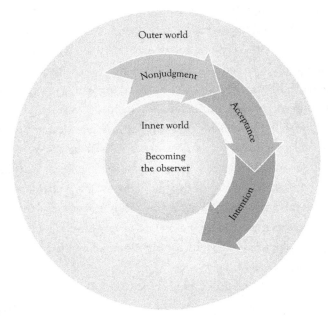

Figure 9.1 Intention

What Is My True Intention

People often say, "My intentions were good" or "I can't believe it was interpreted that way" or "That was not what I meant." Parents will often say to their children or other family members, "But I have your/their best interest in mind, I only want what is best for you." Managers often think they know what is best for their employees.

My concern with these statements is that I don't believe we can ever truly know what is best for another person. Our ego would love us to think that we do, but this kind of thinking gets us into a lot of trouble and is part of the victim mentality culture. I share with you a family-oriented story first in order to have you really internalize the importance of this topic. The complexities around intention require examples that allow the majority of us to relate to then I will bring it back to the work environment.

Many parents believe they know what is best for their young children, especially once they are in the school system. I am not talking about the basic needs for safety, food, and water but things like personal preferences or choices in life. There is often an assumption that children are a blank slate and that the parent is required to teach right and wrong from their perspective. As a result, parents can spend a significant amount of energy trying to influence their children to do what they think is best.

A couple of years ago in one of our Creating Positive Energy: The Science of Well-Being workshops, I was working with a group of people who were not corporate or business leaders but people who simply wanted to learn new skills for resiliency and happiness. When we approached the concept of acceptance, one participant stated that her 16-year-old son had not done well on a science examination and she knew that this was going to potentially impact his overall marks, which he had been monitoring for university entrance. She was visibly uncomfortable with the concept of acceptance. The conversation was very interesting. I asked her permission if she would be willing to share and allow the group to use it as an example. She agreed.

She shared with the group that her son had discovered his gifts for math and science after several years of struggling at school. He was not very social and had trouble fitting in during his formative years. He also struggled with language arts classes. However, when he was about 9 or 10, he discovered that he was pretty good at math and also in the sciences. He really enjoyed biology and chemistry. He was now in Grade 11 and was taking all of the university entrance sciences and math exams. He had recently come home with an important examination mark in biology that was below a C grade and she was very concerned. I asked her to share with the group what her conversation was like with her son. She said, "I asked him why he did so poorly, that I was concerned because he is so much smarter and that I was really concerned he was not meeting his potential." She went on to say that she expressed how good he was in science and that she knew he was so talented. There was no question that she really meant well.

One of the reflection questions that I asked the group was, what was the message her son heard? Not what she said, but what had he heard and more importantly felt? The group carefully stated that he probably heard, "I have let mom down, mom is disappointed in me, I am not good enough, I am going to potentially have additional problems with both my mom and the school." Of course we don't know what he felt or heard but most children in this situation feel exactly that, I have let my parents down. It is very common. I know it is hard to believe but at the core of all young children are humans who want to make mom and dad happy. In many cases they will do anything they can to please their parents until they become so unhappy themselves that they rebel and look for other ways to feel loved and accepted. Children often lose their true selves (nature) trying to please their parents. Parents never intentionally create this environment but it is often a by-product of supposed good intentions. I will often say in these situations that our intentions don't really matter, it is the end result or unintended result that is important. Our ability to stand in the shoes of another person and try to predict how it will feel to receive certain comments or feedback is so critical for anyone in a position of authority. Empathy is the skill of being able to stand in the shoes of another and try to feel the emotions that would occur in certain situations. Because we are all human, we share some common responses to common situations, our ability to take ourselves to a similar emotional situation in order to feel what it might be like for the other person is critical.

How often do we truly take time to stand in the shoes of our employees prior to giving them feedback? I don't mean to simply use our imagination but to try and feel what it will be like for them. This is where removing the manager hat and even sometimes the leader hat to put on the human being hat is so important. Connecting human to human is a critical leadership skill.

It is not uncommon for employees to respond the same way this woman's son would to feedback. Often the threat response occurs. They feel vulnerable and unsure. Employees, for the most part, want to be successful, meet commitments and expectations of their employer, and feel a sense of belonging. However, their version of this might be very different from yours and when we don't monitor our true intention, this is when we can get into trouble.

Let's take a simple example that we have seen in many organizations, especially those struggling to shift to a new energy approach. In this situation there is an employee with poor performance that you have been working hard to manage. Over several months you have been noticing reduced performance, distraction, and what appears to be a lack of commitment. You are spending lots of time trying to manage the situation. You have been using most of the old energy conversations that include telling the person about expectations in order to improve the situation. Performance improves for a couple of weeks and then slowly slides right back. You are getting frustrated, and even somewhat angry. How do you think the employee is feeling? What are they thinking? What emotions and neurochemicals are flowing through their bodies at the anticipation of another conversation with their boss? My suspicion is that some of the negative stress hormones are involved at the thought of being called into the office again. As we already know this can adversely affect how they feel as well as their ability to make good decisions. They begin to anticipate failing. It can be a vicious cycle. In fact, I had one client say, "It feels like the HR walk of shame."

Who Is It About Anyway?

If we go back now to the mom and her son, we can ask some further questions in order to highlight some additional issues around intent.

Who is this issue around the examination mark really about? If we stand in the parent's shoes and really try to feel what it is like for the parent, what do we think might be going on? We might be able to assume that the mom and dad were really happy when they discovered their son's natural aptitude for science and math, especially after a few difficult years of school when marks weren't great and social skills weren't where the system would have wanted them to be. In this specific case it was rather obvious that the parent really wanted their son to be successful. The woman indicated that she hoped her son would go to university and get a degree in science because he was so smart. The real issue was what did her son want?

Often in these simple cases, if we dig really deep and we are really honest, we discover that our actions are more connected to what the parent wants. Parents love to be able to say how smart and capable their kids are, how successful they are, how often they have been on the honor roll. More importantly, when children are successful and get good grades in university and then goods jobs, the parent can begin to relax knowing their child is self-sufficient. The parent can begin to feel a sense of relief. Is it possible that when we truly explore and dig deep, we discover that these issues are more about the parent than about the child? This may not be obvious at first or the parent's conscious intention, yet nevertheless, it's often at the core of the issue.

The parent example is easy for many people to relate to however, sometimes our manager examples are not as easy because we get caught up in the employment contract and we become more mechanical, forgetting that the person is human. I am not suggesting the employment contract isn't important, I am suggesting that the same principles apply because we are dealing with a human, not a machine. When we take the simple performance management issues described above and we ask the manager why are you doing performance management, the answers are usually the same. "It is my job, I am expected to manage the outcomes of my team members. I am expected to manage their performance and behavior." At the extremes we might hear, "My job would get so much easier if my employees would simply do their jobs and meet corporate expectations. My boss would be happy and would stop asking me about this person and what I am doing about it."

So who is this all about? All of the above is about the organization, the manager, and the manager's boss. Rarely is it about the employee. Yet the employee is at the center of the issue and the employee is the only person who can really make the necessary personal changes to improve performance. When we dig deep and really look at the true intention, we discover that the manager's life would be easier if the employee simply met expectations, their boss would be happier and the organization would benefit. Isn't this why the employee is being paid anyway? When we take something that is really human and we make it mechanical, robotic, and policy driven, we unintentionally remove the responsibility and accountability from the employee. We make everything about the company, the department, and the manager, which unfortunately will never help to assist the employee in changing results. It leaves all of the energy and responsibility with the manager.

One of the biggest issues in these scenarios is that the employee and the woman's son feel the true intention, even though the words might not depict this. When the manager feels frustrated with the employee and believes the employee is wasting their valuable time, no matter what the manager says in the meeting, the employee will feel the true intention. Sustainable change cannot occur within a person when the energy (intention) is focused somewhere else. Managers often believe that their employees don't know they are underperforming and it is their job to tell them, however our experience is that deep down inside the employee knows, even though it is not obvious or at the surface.

Leadership Has Everything to Do With the Leader and Nothing to Do With the Leader at the Same Time

When the leader decides to monitor intention all of the time and do the necessary reflection work prior to performance meetings with team members, the results can and do dramatically change. When an employee is underperforming one of the first things we need to do is apply positive regard. What does this mean? It means we assume no negative intentions by the employee. We have positive regard for them. Then the leader asks: Do I have all of the information and do I really know what is going on for this employee? The answer should always be no. You can never truly know what is going on for another person, how they feel, or what they are dealing with. So the leader's challenge is to get to a place where they can acknowledge and remove any negative stories in their head (judgments) about the person and accept the situation and person exactly where they are. Then the leader can ask: What are my intentions when I interact with this person regarding the recent issues? When the leader can step back and do the personal work and reflection knowing that it is not about them, their organization, or their team, they begin to prepare to meet the employee in a very different way.

If the leader does what they have always done, they will get the same results they have always gotten. But when the leader understands the importance of intention, they can reflect and make a shift within themselves. Now the leader's intention could become, I really want this employee to succeed and feel that they belong. I really would like to assist the employee in discovering more about themselves and their work here. I would really like to learn more about the situation from the employee's perspective. It really matters to me that this employee is happy and loves coming to work because I know that happiness and well-being are directly connected to outcomes and it is great to have happy employees. These intentions, when true and authentic, create positive energy that has incredible momentum to create the right dialogue where true sustainable change can occur.

It is important to note that it is not the responsibility of the leader to *make* the employee happy. It is the responsibility of the leader to truly want their team members to be happy. The leader fundamentally changes in order to create the right environment where the meaningful and important exploration and discoveries with the employee can occur. They have done the necessary preparation to ask the right questions in order to assist their team member. You can see that this leadership approach is not for the faint of heart and requires a new and exciting way of interacting human to human instead of boss to subordinate. This is the beginning of creating the right environment where true personal accountability can flourish.

Honesty Before Kindness Always

Another common tool that is explored in detail in the New World Leadership™ programming is Honesty Before Kindness Always. When I first mention this to a new group of leaders, I am often faced with a fabulous discussion around the risks of being honest and that many corporate cultures do not encourage this. Leaders find themselves dancing around issues trying to spare people's feelings, or worse, trying to make a superior happy.

One of my favorite questions to ask executive teams is, "Are you always honest with each other 100 percent of the time?" The initial answer is always, "Yes, of course." Then I will ask, "So you never leave a meeting with something different in your head than what you stated in the room? You never leave with important unsaid things?" This usually gets them thinking. Which of course is all we want to do. The fact is that in most organizations we are still not open, honest, and truthful in many areas.

The simple statement, honesty before kindness always, does not tell the whole story. The only way leaders can be truly honest and create positive outcome is if they have completed a deep and reflective consideration of their intention. If, while being honest, their true intention is to convince others that their views and opinions are the correct ones or to make another person wrong and themselves right, they are not likely to have a meaningful and valuable dialogue. In fact, they are likely to invoke negative emotions and negative responses such as defensiveness, and blaming which of course links to the victim mindset. If we change the statement to "Honesty + Positive Intention = Kindness," we can create a completely different story. We can now create an environment where people feel safe to be honest with one another. If I am honest and have monitored my intention, I am more likely to be successful. For example, if my intention is to share a different viewpoint from a neutral place or to impart additional information, then my intention will be received more openly. If I need to share some observations about performance and my intention is that I truly care about the employee and their success, then I can be honest with positive intention, creating a safe space for the employee to reflect. The employee will feel the leader's positive energy and will be more likely to really reflect and be more open to exploration of the issue.

We desperately need more honesty in the corporate world. Without the key reflection on the leader's intention, we will continue to isolate people and reduce performance due to an ego-based need to be right. Our continued willingness to really do the hard work as leaders is essential to moving into the new energy accountability framework.

Forgiveness

The act of forgiveness is a fundamental tool for the Spiritually Aligned New World Leaders. We have all been wronged at some time or felt that we have been betrayed or disrespected. Some people's stories include very sad and horrific past wrongdoings that make it incredibly difficult for them to forgive. Yet forgiveness is fundamental for leaders and organizations as a whole. Here is a simple example where forgiveness played an important role in a leader's growth and development. A mid-level manager in a large organization came to us for some coaching and discovered quickly that forgiveness was fundamental to his ability to move on and create the career and work life that he truly wanted. Steve had worked for a large organization for over 22 years. The vice president in the area in which he worked had personally asked him to take a lateral management position to assist the company with a very challenging situation. Steve had been called upon in the past to assist the corporation and each time he had agreed. Steve knew the department in question and he was not really interested in this opportunity. The work itself was not something Steve felt was challenging and he knew the department had lots of systemic issues.

He wanted the vice president to know that he would take this new lateral role and help the company out but that he wanted to be considered for the next director position that came available. A straightforward and candid individual, Steve came right out and told the vice president that he was very interested in a director role (promotion) and felt that he was ready. The vice president agreed that he would consider Steve for a future promotion and so Steve accepted the assignment, even though the work was not what he really wanted.

Steve worked in this new role for about 18 months, fixing the problems and performing as expected by his boss. As a very driven and accomplished leader, Steve was ready to get the next promotion. He felt he had done everything right and was absolutely shocked, angered, and frustrated when the director position he had been working toward was given to another leader. He was not even asked to apply. The anger that Steve felt toward his organization was very strong, and he began to disengage. He went from being a high-performing leader to a disengaged manager who felt great resentment toward his organization, he began to look outside the company for employment. It is at this point Steve came to us looking for assistance.

Let's take a look at what could have happened had Steve not worked on forgiveness. The vice president would have lost a great leader, Steve would have lost his fabulous tenure with the organization, and the company would have lost some long-term intellectual property.

Two things occurred for Steve during our coaching work which were pivotal in his journey to becoming a better leader. Before agreeing to take the lateral position, Steve was in a role that he absolutely loved. It was challenging, he was working with great people, had tons of autonomy, and was valued as a key contributor. So why would he leave and go to the new lateral management position that he knew he didn't want? When I asked him why he took the position he said, "Because they were willing to consider me for the next promotion." Then I asked, "When they initially came to you with the proposal, did they mention you would be given the next director role?" Steve answered, "No, I was the one that brought it up."

It's possible the vice president said what Steve wanted to hear in an effort to get Steve to agree to help him out but what's more important is the fact that Steve allowed his ego to make his decisions, not his heart. Steve knew from the beginning that he didn't want the role but he decided that if he could get the director position in a year or two, it was worth it. By settling for the needs of the ego, Steve became completely attached to the idea that he would be the next director but when the time came, Steve was overlooked.

As we talked further, Steve could clearly recall knowing inside that the role was not a good fit for him and that he really didn't want it. The result of not listening to that intuitive heart-centered inner voice was that he was stuck doing work he really didn't enjoy.

There are two main reasons why situations like Steve's continue to occur in organizational life. The first is that leaders and managers are not in alignment. Often senior leaders dictate the organizational alignment and it stands to follow that when these senior leaders are not in alignment, the organization cannot be. The second reason is best illustrated by what happened when I asked Steve why he wanted the specific director position. He couldn't give a definite answer as to why that position was so important. In our work together he was honest enough to admit that it was not the role and the specific work that attracted him, but the possible new promotion. He realized what was at play in these scenarios, ego. The vice president was also not in alignment because he was not in a position to lead Steve to believe that he would be considered for the director position. He could not have known what the future would hold and therefore if he had been completely honest with Steve, he would have told him this. His ego was also at play, working to solve a problem in the quickest and easiest way, even if it meant misalignment.

As I continued to work with Steve and ask him questions, he realized that first he needed to forgive himself for not listening to that inner voice, and then he needed to forgive the vice president. Steve invited that situation into his life and had to take ownership of it if he was going to move on successfully. Steve realized that he was now disengaged from work, not aligned with either himself or his organization, and that people around him knew it. Steve's next task was to go inside and truly listen for the answers. One of the answers was to recognize and take responsibility for the situation. He needed to own his important role in this situation. This would be the beginning of his ability to move on and make better choices for himself and for the organization.

Organizations need engaged and Spiritually Aligned Leaders who listen to their internal guidance and who are not afraid to act on that information. Leaders and employees need to do work that is in alignment with their interests, passions, and organizational goals. Steve was able to tap into the tools of the Accountability Model, observing the negative thoughts he had and the negative feelings they were creating. He was also able to recognize how it was impacting his performance and would ultimately negatively impact him. Then he had to accept things the way they were. Negatively judging his boss for the way things transpired did not serve Steve in any way and so he needed to monitor and observe his judgments and make different choices. Once he did this, he could begin to forgive both himself and the vice president.

As Steve began to forgive the vice president, he was now in a position to consider what he had learned through this event. Could he actually turn his anger to forgiveness and his forgiveness into gratitude? Could he become grateful to the vice president for teaching him this fabulous lesson about ego and the importance of listening to intuition?

I have coached individuals for many years that have been impacted by aggressive bullying behavior in the workplace and the power of forgiveness is so important. In order for a person who is impacted by this extremely negative and disrespectful behavior to move on and become an empowered and a self-responsible contributor, they must work with the tools of the Accountability Model to create forgiveness. Sometimes creating empathy and understanding for the perpetrator is essential. With the knowing that those who hurt people are hurting themselves, we can begin the process of understanding. We acknowledge that what they did will never be OK; however, making the commitment to feel better with positive emotions is essential for those impacted. In order to take their own power back, they must first understand that they are responsible for what they think and feel. They must step away from the victim mentality knowing that it will never serve them because of the negative emotions attached. If they want to feel better, they must change what they think about the situation and the emotions that result.

There seems to be a common belief that forgiveness is about the perpetrator, and that the victim needs to find a way to make what happened OK. Nothing could be further from the truth. We need to understand that the act of forgiveness heals and frees the person who does the forgiving, the focus is within and not necessarily on the perpetrator. Most people will never forget and completely let go of the damages created by a very negative relationship. However, in the right context, we can find ways to shift the energy around these events to one of healing and personal transformation. The events can become catalysts that propel us forward in a positive way. I have witnessed very difficult and harmful anger that moves to empathy, then understanding, acceptance, forgiveness, and eventually gratitude. The person internalizes the value of the experience, the significant learning opportunity and benefits from true growth and evolution.

Forgiveness brings amazing gifts to the forgiver, relief that could never be felt without a full and complete understanding of the intense value of forgiveness. You have to be willing to look for the signs. You have to observe and monitor your thoughts around these negative situations and ask yourself: Are my thoughts good feeling thoughts? Do my thoughts serve me in a positive way? Leaders and employees who feel they have been wronged benefit greatly when they begin to ask these important questions. It is then that you are able to begin to consider forgiveness, which frees the person and allows them to move on with positive energy and heightened empowerment.

Summary

As you are probably beginning to see, most of the work required to create this new energy environment of accountability initially lies with the leader. Leaders must be the change that they want to see and feel within the workplace. When leaders are conscious, present minded, and deliberate in everything they do, they begin to create the new environment which naturally builds momentum toward self-responsibility.

One of the comments we often get is, "How much work this is?" Leaders simply don't have time to slow down and do this personal work. My question is always the same, "How much time in any given week or month are you spending managing performance of individual team members? How much time in any given week or month, are you dealing with conflict and interpersonal relationship or miscommunication issues? What if most or all of the issues were gone, how much time would that free up for you to work *on* the business instead of *in* the business?" These are the powerful questions. Everything worth creating takes positive intention and attention along with a commitment of time. The rewards are astounding and the results do not take long to be noticeable.

CHAPTER 10

Detachment and Unconditional Positive Regard

Applying the tool of detachment continues to be the hardest skill I practice each day and the hardest skill for leaders to accept and to commit to practice. This single attribute and process of the Accountability Model faces greater resistance than all others. This is because we are trained from very early on that there is right and wrong, good and bad, nice people and not nice people. We are conditioned as leaders to judge everything. This trains us to be attached to the outcomes that our direct reports provide to the team and to us personally. We have expectations and believe we have a right to have expectations. Shedding these beliefs is the one true attribute that will accelerate the adoption of personal accountability within your team faster than any of the other tools. But as always, it begins with you the leader. Figure 10.1 depicts the next phase in the Accountability Model: Detachment. The real irony of this technique is that you almost have to *not* care about the results in order to truly and wholeheartedly care about the results. I know that this may not make sense yet, but stay with it as this concept is so important.

It requires discipline and a knowing that this is exactly how life is supposed to be. We are supposed to detach so that we can experience unconditional positive regard for others. This allows people to truly own the results they get, regardless of whether they are positive or negative, and whether we agree or disagree. It is impossible for a leader to create a culture of true individual accountability if they spend most of their time worrying about others and having opinions and views of how others should conduct themselves. Why would you want to spend time on something you have no control over? Unconditional positive regard is

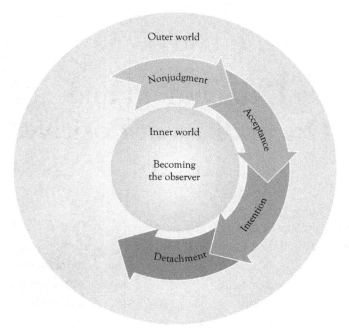

Figure 10.1 Detachment

the care and compassion that arises as a result of accepting and caring for others just as they are, even when you disagree with them. It is absolutely OK to acknowledge that you would not do something yourself that someone else has done, as this is free will and choice, but to judge it and apply negative emotion is to create attachment. The leader still owns the issue or situation when they have an attachment to the results. The leader gets stuck on what they think should happen, leaving most of the energy with the leader. Detachment allows us to find that sweet spot of true unconditional care and compassion that creates an empowering level of freedom and personal responsibility for the other person. Remember, telling someone they have to be accountable does not work, in the long run, but creating the right environment through your own self-leadership and detachment can have the exact results you are looking for and can truly help the other person shift if they so choose.

Detachment can be applied in several ways and for the purposes of the Accountability Model, I will share the two most common ways. The first is that of detaching from what others believe, feel, and do. The second application is the ability to detach from how and when results manifest. Detaching from outcomes is really hard in the corporate environment but this is in fact exactly how we get great results. When we simply let go, we create an amazing environment where others begin to do their personal work and where they have to take responsibility for their outcomes because no one else will do that for them.

Everything Is Upside Down

The challenge with trying to create this culture in the dense and mechanistic hierarchical structures of old energy organizations is that these structures are actually upside down, they are keeping all of the power and responsibility with a few people at the top. Our old energy systems want us to believe that we will get optimal performance when the people at the top tell the people "lower down" what to do and hold them accountable. It is a fallacy. This simply serves to frustrate everyone. You cannot tell someone to take responsibility. True responsibility comes from the inside out, not from the outside in.

Here is the easiest way to reflect on this. Frontline employees know that their supervisor is responsible for the day-to-day production and that the supervisor is responsible to the manager and the manager responsible to the director and the director to the vice president. Subconsciously, frontline employees know that ultimately they have very little power and control over their day. Yet control over one's day is essential to one's well-being. Often frontline employees don't even know why they are so frustrated. Usually the victim mentality will be the strongest at the frontline and will still be visible at the supervisor and manager level. This makes sense. The less-perceived control a person has over their day, the more likely they will feel out of personal alignment and the more they begin to feel like an insignificant cog in a wheel. All of the responsibility is perceived, whether true or not, to be held by a small group at the top of an organization. This is not how to create a culture of accountability.

I am not suggesting that we remove the hierarchical nature of business, as there is always someone who has to sign the check and make final decisions where appropriate. I am suggesting that we view our hierarchies differently and, most importantly, we begin to *treat* them differently. One of the primary roles and responsibilities of senior leaders is to create an accountability culture through practicing the tools, techniques, and process that lead to a more authentic, genuine, and humanistic approach to decision making, problem solving, and overall effort. Leaders simply know and believe that each person is responsible and so this is the energy they put out.

A common statement you might hear in organizations that create this culture of accountability is,

> I follow the policies and rules out of respect for the company, not because compliance is expected. In fact, I know that if I deviate from a rule or policy, because it is the right thing to do (aligns with our compelling purpose and values of the organization), the company will always support me. They want me to feel comfortable making decisions as long as they align with the corporate purpose and values.

In this situation, the power and control is in a very different place. It is not with the supervisor, manager, or director but with a frontline employee who is trusted and cared for enough to know that it is OK to make a decision, as long as it leans in the direction of the organization's values and purpose.

The reason this environment is so hard to create is that senior leaders often lead from a place of fear of losing control, fear of not knowing every detail, and fear of not being in a position to understand every situation in the organization. We often see organizations being led by a small group of leaders who may not realize the ego is in large part controlling things. They have not done their personal leadership work. There is a reason people feel they are not trusted. It is because we unintentionally teach them they are not trusted. Not being trusted invokes the fight or flight response, which we know impacts our thought processes and decision making. It is also important to note that these senior leaders are not intentionally controlling and fear based, they feel a huge sense of responsibility, which is also a result of our past, old energy structures and history.

What if CEOs could actually feel like they were in this together with great competent people who simply want to do their best? This belief is possible and provides significant relief for the leader as it opens the leader up to viewing the senior team quite differently and, more importantly, fosters a new respect for their frontline. Of course not all CEOs are controlling and fear based. However those that are, usually have no idea that they are leading from a place of fear, resulting in a need for control and a message of low trust. One of the major challenges we see is that when a CEO has all the right skills, they may have vice presidents who don't. If the compelling purpose and leadership values are not upheld, it sometimes doesn't matter how great the CEO is if others are not in true alignment with the organization's guiding principles. This is so important. In this case, vice presidents that are stuck in the old energy are no different than those at the mid-level, they need to do their own personal work in order to shift. When building these dynamic accountability cultures, we quickly lose credibility if we leave leaders, who are stuck and unwilling to do their work, in their roles for long.

As we create a culture of accountability, the triangle becomes inverted with the masses taking responsibility for their small and yet important individual role in the corporation. Teams begin to view responsibility and accountability differently and the victim mentality fades away.

Detachment Is Not Disengagement

We often ask leaders to tell us the difference between detachment and disengagement. This is a valuable exercise as it helps us reflect on the importance of detachment without feeling we need to stop caring.

Disengagement is when a person gives up. When an employee states, "I don't care" sometimes what they are really saying is, "I really care but have given up." This is disengagement. They go through the motions, they show up but don't really have their mind or heart on the job. It becomes a means to an end. There is usually a lot of negative emotion attached to disengagement.

Detachment does not have any negative emotion connected to it. It is a person's ability to accept things as they are without a negative response. Sometimes it is easier to provide a personal example before we look at the work context. The personal examples can assist us in processing these tools because it is OK to be more accepting of emotions in our personal lives. We have been taught to disregard emotions in the workplace. This gets us in trouble every time because the emotions are still there. They are just buried where we think no one can see them. Buried emotions eventually show up in behavior and often others can feel your emotions, even if you are not speaking your mind.

Let's go back to our mother with the son who was strong in science and math. This mother was attached to the outcomes of her son doing well in school so that he could go on to a successful university life. Those attachments create certain emotions, which create certain energies, which impact her ability to have the discussion with her son that would be most helpful. It impacts her behavior. But when she can use the Accountability Model and its processes, she can intellectually and emotionally begin to view the entire situation differently. She can be honest with herself about why she is attached to a certain outcome. She can begin to accept that her son's life is *his* life, not hers. Then she can create a safe environment where he can explore what he wants, make individual choices and take responsibility for those choices without feeling judged. He begins to be the owner of his life. She must do her own work first and foremost in order to create the right environment so that he can own his own results.

What if her son becomes a plumber and loves being a plumber, or a city worker planting flowers in the park? Why should any of this matter to her? When she can detach and not make it about the ultimate outcomes that she wants, she can begin to ask totally different questions to assist her son in exploring what he truly wants and what really makes him happy. When she is attached and has emotions associated with the end result, her son can feel this. This impacts his ability to openly explore his own feelings because he is trying so hard to make someone else happy. It becomes about the mom not about the son.

Mom does not become disengaged with her son and his education but becomes detached in order to make it about him, his needs, wants, and desires. She is now coming from a true place of love and acceptance. When children are given the space and time to explore what they want, desire and need without the heavy influence of mom and dad, they become responsible and accountable for their actions and results. They do not leave home feeling victimized by their well-intending parents, but feel genuinely loved and cared for just as they are, with no sense that they need to be a certain way. This is how unconditional love emerges. It is not about not caring! It is about caring enough to do the hard work of detaching to allow the other person time and space to find their own truth and alignment. All of the same principles apply in our working world and interpersonal relationships.

Detaching From the Outcomes of Others

As a leader in the corporate world, detaching from the outcomes of others is completely counterintuitive. We have all been trained to believe that we are accountable for the outcomes of other people and that our job is to manage those outcomes. However, it is this core belief that holds us back from creating a true culture of accountability. You want the employee to be fully committed to the results they get and to feel fully accountable. The only way to do this is to not be accountable and attached to the results for them, but to create the environment where the employee learns they have no other choice but to take their power back, to own the results they get and that the victim mentality is not an option. This is the real transformational shift needed to create amazing results.

Now let's take a professional example and apply it the same way. When we have attachments to how our employees perform, we also have emotions relating to these outcomes. We have stories of good and bad, right and wrong and we become emotionally attached to how people perform. This becomes so evident with leaders when they are trying to influence a contributor's performance. They will call them into the office and begin to share with them what they have observed. Everything starts out well intended. Soon the leader begins to share their expectations of the employee. They give examples of the employees observed behavior, which is often in direct contradiction to what the leader expects. The employee sits and listens to the leader explain what they need and want from them and what the team and organization are expecting. Of course, good managers will also throw in some questions for the employee about their work and work process, but more importantly the leader is focused on sharing their expectations. Our experience is that the manager does about 80 percent of the talking. The employee feels the attachment and energy of the manager and subconsciously notes the manager's level of responsibility to the outcome, their attachments. The leader owns the conversation and holds the energy.

In many cases the employee sits dutifully in the chair across from their manager waiting for it to all be over or waiting to get a word in, waiting to be heard. When the employee does not have to do any talking, share their views and concerns, process intellectually the situation, or even reflect on other viewpoints, they get away with little or no internal sense of responsibility. In fact, they often leave the meeting subconsciously sensing or knowing that the manager is responsible. They have not had to process because the leader has done all of the processing for them. They can quickly assume the victim role. The employee's behavior may change for a very short time out of fear but there is no long-lasting impact from the discussion because there has been no internal shift or change within the employee. They sense that it is not theirs but the manager's issue (energy).

Now let's apply the tools and specifically the ability to detach from the outcomes. The leader must first recognize that they do not know the employee fully and that they only have information from a small vantage point. When the leader can detach from the outcome of the meeting and recognize that the issue is not theirs but the employee's, then they can begin to manage their emotions, expectations, and intention. The leader enters a meeting from a place of curiosity, exploration and, hopefully, discovery. The leader has no expectation of a specific outcome. This is so important because it informs the leader on what questions to ask and how to approach the conversation. It removes the emotions (energy) that say, I am responsible for getting you to do your job. The employee feels the difference right away. The focus is on the employee, what they think, feel, and are experiencing. The leader attempts to stand in the shoes of the employee with a true willingness to learn from the employee, making the employee the expert in their own life and career. This creates a space for true exploration by the employee that can include reflection, intellectual processing and identification of their own story, judgments, and emotions. This is when change can begin to take form. The authentic and meaningful conversation can now begin where powerful questions and intense listening become the final tools of the leader. In the background, the leader knows where they must take the team and the results they are looking for but they also know that the individual team members are the only ones that can decide to come along with positive commitment and responsibility for results. The leader can neither do this for them nor should they want to. The leader creates the right environment where the employees can truly make a commitment for themselves.

It is important for leaders to recognize they cannot always assist every contributor in their journey to full accountability. Some will be very stuck in the old energy with a victim mentality and do not know any other way. In fact, many can become addicted to the negative emotions and resulting hormones. In these cases, it can be very difficult as the leader realizes they may not be able to assist the person in creating new neural connections. This is usually a very small percentage of the team; however, it does happen. We will review the can't and won't model in a later chapter to explain this progression and the process that can be used in this situation.

When the leader is detached from outcomes, they can truly hear the employee, be present and intentional in their listening. The experience is significantly different for the employee. If done right, the employee will often leave that first meeting wondering what just happened because they are so used to an expectations-based conversation where all of the focus is on the manager, team, and organizational expectations.

Detaching From What Others Think and Feel

The other side of this intentional tool is the ability to detach from what others think or feel about you. Many of us spend a significant amount of time thinking and worrying about whether we make others happy, whether we meet their expectations. Many of our coaching clients believe that they are not trying to make others happy, but as we ask questions and they explore their feelings, they discover that at the core of their concerns are their attempts at trying to constantly meet others' expectations.

As a leader, monitoring how much you value the opinions and views of others is important. Yes, you want to be open to learn and understand the views of others but you need to also be aware of what feels right for you. Leaders are often heavily influenced by their boss. They are watching, learning, and adapting to their boss' style. This is good in order to connect with them better, as long as it feels right and balanced. However, sometimes a manager will be so heavily influenced by their leader, they will continuously do things they feel are wrong but do it out of a sense of obligation or fear. This is where personal alignment is at risk and the leader is more likely to make mistakes and produce less than great work due to the negative emotions associated with being out of alignment.

Detaching does not mean that you detach from your own emotions. It means you compromise and let go of things you cannot control. However, if you are in a situation where you are continuously out of alignment, your reflections should be more on how you can move from that situation into a healthier one. If you can do this with no judgment and with acceptance for your current situation, you are likely to recognize that you are simply in the wrong role with the wrong company. You can process your negative emotions, take responsibility for the situation you are in, detach and know that it is only a moment in time and that you can shift your thinking, which will change your feelings, emotions, and behaviors. When you do your own work you create the best possibilities to manifest a new situation and new opportunities that are more aligned to what you want and need. My experience is that leaders who are clearly in the wrong role and do not do their own important work first, run to a new employer, and find themselves in the same situation with the same issues.

Guilt is another emotion that has no place in our lives. It is the one emotion that serves no purpose and needs to be monitored and observed carefully. When a person does something out of guilt or out of a need to make another person happy, the results are often more negative emotions such as resentment and frustration. If these emotions are suppressed, over time they will manifest into bad behavior. We all have experienced guilt and have done something only because someone else wanted us to and in the end we didn't feel good.

Some of these situations can include decisions made at the senior level that you are required to implement. You may disagree with the decision but feel obligated out of a sense of loyalty to your employer or fear of reprisal. Old energy organizations train their leaders to simply show support, even if they don't agree. They are told it is their responsibility to deliver the news and implement regardless of personal feelings. Be very careful with these situations because when you think you are hiding your true thoughts, feelings, and emotions on a topic, you are not. Your employees will be able to feel your negative emotions regardless of your message. Your credibility and authenticity are at stake.

In important situations like these, using the tools of the Accountability Model is crucial. Ask yourself why you really disagree and then ask yourself, why again. Recognize and be honest about your emotions and judgments about the situation. Ask yourself: Do I have all of the information or is this simply my ego believing I know what is best? When you go through the process of understanding your judgments, accepting things as they are and really understanding your own intentions, you will probably find that you can successfully detach and deliver the information and answer questions from an authentic and credible place.

Of course, if you are working for an employer that you regularly feel out of alignment from and it gets harder and harder to support their approach, then different decisions need to be made. In a situation like this it is even more important that you use these tools and techniques. You do not want to leave angry or upset, managing your emotions is critical in order to make great decisions and to land your next opportunity with grace, balance, and positive energy.

Summary

Although detachment seems very counterintuitive, the results we get when we are able to detach are amazing. We care more, we ask better questions, we explore topics more openly, and we discover new things about old situations.

Detachment allows the leader to authentically turn the attention toward the employee in a meaningful way. The employee can begin to do his or her own self-exploration and reflection. This is where the magic begins. The leader becomes the catalyst for open discussion about growth and development, performance, and behavior simply because they care enough to detach and focus on the employee and not on the needs of the team or organization.

Once the leader has detached and recognizes that the only person who can change the employee's trajectory is the employee, the leader can feel a sense of relief and create a different relationship with the employee. The leader goes through the process and stages of creating the Accountability

Culture and then assists the employee in doing the same thing. When employees learn how to monitor judgments through observation and role models and to accept things as they are, they can begin to monitor their own intentions and attachments. The leader becomes an amazing coach that knows how to create the safe space for the employee to make their own decisions regarding contribution, employment, commitment, and accountability. I have seen how powerful this process is and how it changes lives, both professionally and personally.

CHAPTER 11

The Coaching Conversation

All of the previous chapters have been about the leader doing their personal and important work first in order to shift the long-held beliefs about management, performance, accountability, and outcomes. This chapter provides the next layer in moving the responsibility from the leader to the employee. Figure 11.1 provides a visual of the coaching component in The Accountability Model. It is very strategically placed here to ensure that the leader does there own personal work prior to engaging in the coaching conversation.

There have been many great books written about coaching and the coaching conversation over the past 15 years. Unfortunately some leaders move right to coaching and creating questions when they themselves have

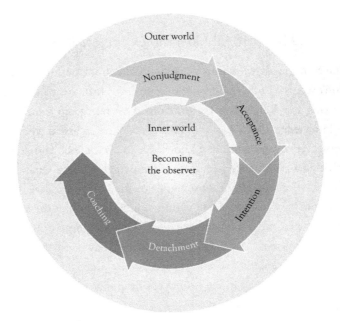

Figure 11.1 Coaching

not done the critical work of shifting their belief system about themselves and their employees. As a quick review, the majority of our employees, even those fully entrenched in the victim mentality, want to belong, want to do good work, and be appreciated for that work. Most importantly they deeply want some level of control over their day. When we can sit quietly, reflect and recognize that our systems, structures, and past beliefs have created the cultures we now work in, we can begin to build some empathy and better understanding for the employees that struggle. Both the organization and the leaders can own a portion of the responsibility for the less than great corporate cultures and resulting outcomes. It seems counterintuitive but when we give employees the right opportunities to take responsibility for themselves, they get relief and clarity that they may not have felt in some time. In short, when you the leader are on a personal journey of unlearning the last 100 years of mechanistic management approaches you will get amazing relief, closer alignment to who you really are, better access to your intuition and gut feel, and will be able to lead from a place of unconditional care and concern. You gain all of this without ever taking the responsibility for the results of another person. It truly works!

The Critical Coaching Conversation

You have an employee who is struggling with poor performance. They just don't seem to understand what the company, team, or you, the leader, are looking for. Rarely is a performance issue related to a lack of cognitive knowledge about the job. Take some time to assess whether you have observed a genuine lack of knowledge to do the job. More often the underlying cause is related to an attitude or belief about their work or working relationships. Your sense might be they just don't care. If that is the case, you have just identified your first judgment about the employee. You may have some observable evidence that would lead you to believe the employee doesn't care however, remember that bad behavior, like a lack of caring, is not natural but learned. Something has happened along the way to create a story in the employee's head that reduced their level of care and concern for quality work.

Usually our organizations invest significant money and time in the recruitment and selection process as well as all of the training that occurs after the hiring process. When that much time and energy is invested in hiring an employee, each and every one deserves the opportunity to understand why he or she has stopped caring and to decide if they want to choose a different path. As we know through the study of neuroscience, everyone has the capability to rewire their brain once they make the decision to.

As the leader, you consider all of your judgments about this employee and decide that you need to reflect on the stories you have about the situation. You ask yourself all of the hard questions. Do I have all of the information? Do I truly know this employee? The answers are always, no. Accepting the person right where they are and reminding yourself that they probably want to do a good job and want to belong and be part of the team will all help in building positive energy. This is the state of positive regard for others. Then you get very clear about your intentions. Sometimes using a simple imagination game helps leaders to visualize a new and improved situation. You imagine what it will be like, feel like, when each and every employee takes responsibility for their outcomes. You imagine what it will be like when employees are honest and open when things were not going well, and feel totally safe to tell you the brutal truth. These same employees seek feedback about their performance without you giving feedback unsolicited. This can be the new paradigm. You apply all of these techniques to the specific employee that has struggling performance.

You then completely detach from the outcomes and know that you are going to quietly and safely place the responsibility on the other side of the table through great questions that are compassionate and well thought out. Knowing that your shift in awareness and accountability took some time means that you will be more willing to give your employees time to reflect and make changes. You may also decide that the first couple of meetings will be brief and there will be no expectations or actions requested from the employee. Imagine having a completely exploratory discussion with your team member without asking for anything in return. You don't request that they do anything different, you don't request they change their behavior. You simply explore the topic with open, nonjudg-mental positive regard for the other person.

When we ask leaders what they think will happen if they do this they often say, "The employee will think I am crazy! They will think that I have lost my marbles." When we ask why they say, "Because we never have coaching meetings without asking for a change in outcome or behavior. That's my job. The employee will simply be shocked by the nature of the discussion. They may not know what to do with it." The fact that the employee is shocked or surprised by this approach is a good thing. It means that they will reflect on what just happened. After the first conver-sation, they may wonder whether their leader was truly interested in them and how they feel. How do you think the employee will feel coming to the second meeting knowing how the first meeting went?

We usually get two different answers here. One, the employee will most likely be more open, more trusting, and simply more relaxed at the second and third meeting. Two, the employee is going to have heightened trust issues, will be suspicious and less likely to share anything in the second meeting. This second response is usually a sign of a dysfunctional, nontrusting environment where employees are in heightened states of vic-tim consciousness. Fear is at the core of their emotional state at work and they simply can't imagine a leader caring enough about them to have a genuine conversation where the focus is on them and how they feel. They can't fathom that their leader did not do all the talking and ask for the usual behavior change.

The Powerful Questions—In the Beginning

At first, creating questions can seem like an arduous task full of stress and worry. It can be overwhelming in the beginning. However, the more you do your own work and focus on your own truth and alignment, the more your intuitive self will come through to help guide your question-ing. In the beginning we recommend that you take the manager hat and even the leader hat off and you simply focus on the human-to-human conversation. This is so important when setting the foundation for a new relationship.

There are a couple of things to consider as you begin to create questions. Some of your employees are stuck in the old energy, just like many managers. They have a story in their head about you and the organization. This story creates feelings and emotions that affect their behavior. When you can stand in their shoes for a moment and ask yourself, "I wonder what it is like for them, doing their prescribed work each day, under my leadership," and you are willing to be honest about that answer, you build some awareness prior to creating questions. In the beginning your role is to explore with the employee what is going on from their perspective, not yours. Sharing your long monologue about what you see happening is not going to create the environment you want. Questions can be as simple as, "How have things been going for you lately?" Depending on the specific situation, you will design your language and approach very intentionally. We recommend that in the early days, you write out the questions you might want to ask. Review the questions for ordering and know that you will have to be flexible along the way. If your organization has invested in a strong and comprehensive leadership development program where you have solid knowledge of psychometric assessments and tools for recognizing different preferences, you will be able to consider whether the person is introverted or extroverted. This will help you determine how they might respond to specific questions and how you might want to manage your own energy. If you are working with someone who is introverted, you want to be especially careful not to back them into a corner for quick answers. Be willing to give them time to reflect and get back to you on some of the more difficult questions. This respects their natural preference and they will greatly appreciate it. You are building trust. If the person is extroverted, you might be able to have a longer discussion in the first meeting. Understanding your own style and approach is critical in order to adapt to the employee's preference. Remember, this meeting is not about you, the team, or the organization, but about the employee.

The questions can be as vast and various as there are employees and situations, so it is impossible for me to provide you an extensive list. I always recommend having some specific training on creating the coaching conversation. However, as noted in previous chapters, a coaching program in isolation without the necessary foundational work is usually not effective. Coaching is a natural part of any great leadership development initiative.

Soft Versus Sharp Questions

During the first and second conversations, it is important to begin to ask more direct and thought-provoking questions in order to ensure reflection is occurring. Every situation is completely different and requires a unique approach. Your goal is to discover new things about the person and the situation and then ask questions that build new awareness within yourself and the other person. As you explore the specific issue you can share with the person your observations, but you do this from a detached, objective viewpoint, in a way that truly assists them in staying open to hearing another perspective. Begin your question with "Is it possible that ..." or, "I wonder if ..." At this point you are really beginning to focus on the issues and create a space for the other person to explore how their feelings, thoughts, and emotions are impacting things. This also allows them to consider how others might perceive their behavior. You don't want to tell them, "This is the way it is." You simply want to ask them to consider or reflect on different possibilities. When you do this, you keep the responsibility on the other side of the table. It also keeps the person open with less stress. Less stress and anxiety, as noted in earlier chapters, means more effective processing of information.

We provide the leaders we work with an exercise where they take a series of questions that could be perceived by the other person as sharp or prickly and we ask them to rewrite these questions to be more soft and open. This exercise is powerful in assisting leaders to feel and see the difference and to evaluate their questions as they move along in the process. A simple example might be, "Why did you do ...?" This will feel like it has a judgment attached to it, especially if you are dealing with a person who is at the victim level. A simple change to, "What decision-making criteria did you use when you ...?" This question is far more powerful as it asks the person to provide the process they used to determine the action they took. This question *feels* more open and less judgmental. It creates more curiosity and opportunity for reflection. It also helps to build awareness in the other person. In order to answer the question, they have to relive their process. A second question to follow up on this might be, "How do you think others might have perceived this?" If the person says, "I have no idea," you could follow up with a questions that starts with, "Is it possible that …?" In this scenario you can provide some information but allows the dialogue to continue to be open to exploration.

Sometimes you will work with a person who is really stuck. If you have had one or two meetings and the person is unwilling to consider other perspectives or alternatives, then we often find that asking a sharp question is imperative. We don't recommend this unless necessary. An example might be, "Is it possible that you were really hurt at the time that you said/did what you did and that there may have been a better way to approach it?" or, "Is it possible that you became overly emotional and your ego was triggered?" I always ask, "Are you sure you have all of the information, I wonder if you are only seeing this situation from your perspective?" Talk about honest questioning. Yes, these are prickly questions and questions I would not consider asking until I had met with the person a few times and had tried different approaches. I often preclude this type of sharp question with something like,

> In order for me to understand the situation better and for you to consider alternative approaches, we have had a few conversations about this situation. I sense that you might be really stuck in your position and unwilling to consider possible different approaches and your impact on the situation.

If the leader has done their personal work, created positive intention, and their energy is focused on the other person, they can usually ask these types of candid questions as a way of creating space where the person can reflect. The questions are honest, clear, and deliberate. These questions are not asked with emotion or within a heated debate. They are meaningful, come with positive regard, love, and compassion and in a true effort to be a mirror for the other person. The energy behind the question is of utmost importance as it will impact body language. With the right energy, a true sense that the leader cares will emerge, even when asking these tough questions. It's all about intent. When you really care about a person you can ask the tough questions with compassion and positive regard, not judgment and frustration.

Don't Take the Monkey, It's Not Yours

In many performance management models we have taught leaders to say *we* in order not to have the other person feel supported and not alone. We actually recommend that this be used very sparingly. The reason for this is: Who usually owns the issue? If you are dealing with someone who has had a long-term behavior that is unwanted and negative, then the last thing you want to say is, "How can we help, what can we do?" This simply prolongs joint ownership and joint responsibility. I know it sounds insensitive but if the leader's intentions are held with positive regard toward the employee and the focus is where it needs to be, you can be candid and clear with love and compassion. We want to remember that each individual person is responsible for his or her own behavior, regardless of the situation. That doesn't mean we are insensitive. It means we want to leave the responsibility (issue/problem/monkey) squarely where it belongs, with the other person. If we use *we* language, we lump everyone together and the employee does not have to own his or her own behavior. Asking, "What do you think you want to do about ..." or "What do you think you might do differently if you had the chance," are all great questions that clearly leave the responsibility with the employee.

As a cautionary note, we have a lot of experience with leaders who believe that all issues stem from within the employees. We often discover that the leader's style and approach can be at the root of the issue. One of the clear examples we see quite frequently are leaders who are perfectionists with extremely high standards. They like to use the word *quality* when describing their approach but when they dig deep, it is their perfectionistic tendency combined with very high standards. They work harder than everyone else and often have unrealistic expectations of their team members. Because they are perfectionists and like things done a very specific way, they will often redo their contributors work and red pen things continuously. Remember, we train people how to treat us. In situations like this, team members will either work really hard trying to meet the standard but will always feel inferior or eventually they will simply provide mediocre work knowing the leader will redo it all. The employee quickly takes the victim role. This situation exists in most organizations to different degrees. Trust is low, connection is low and often a complete lack of understanding ensues.

However, in new energy organizations leaders accept that each and every person must be responsible for his or her own behavior. Leaders who are self-aware and honest about their impact on others can certainly ask questions around what it is like to work for them and what they might do differently in order to make it easier or build better relationships. But they won't mix the issues of the employees' behavior with their behavior. They realize that each person must own their own reaction to situations and outcomes. When each party is doing the necessary reflection and creating personal development strategies for enhanced effectiveness, it is a recipe for success. Own your own monkeys while being careful not to take the monkeys of other people, especially your team members. Ask questions that clearly leave the responsibility for reflection and solution with the other person. Know what is yours and do your own work to improve your relationships.

Can't and Won't

One of our clients has a great model that reflects the important shift from *can't* to *won't* and how to integrate the old systems with a new one. In Figure 11.2, the *can't* and *won't* model shown, reflects the importance of knowing we can use both the new tools and techniques but also transition

Figure 11.2 Can't and Won't

back to traditional performance management and progressive discipline when needed. Often employees with performance concerns can't make the shift on their own as they simply don't have the tools and are so conditioned to play the victim role. It is also important to note that creating a culture of accountability is not about everyone being friends and allowing employees, who are stuck, to remain in the victim mentality. Our focus must remain on creating optimal performance through positive energy.

When the leaders of an organization make a collective decision to apply new energy and focus on their own leadership development, they begin to create a trusting environment where employees will see and feel the difference. As the leader begins to change the conversation to one of coaching, exploration, and discovery, they should see a shift in the energy of the employees. Employees should begin to take responsibility. However, there are cases where an employee is so stuck and unwilling to reflect and consider options that even when we have created the right environment there is no shift. In these cases, there is often a lot of anger and well-established blaming on the part of the employee. This is when we move from *can't* to *won't*. The only process left for the leader is our traditional performance management and progressive discipline process. This is not a bad thing. In fact, it is imperative that once an organization makes the commitment to shift to new energy they make no apologies when they need to make the hard decisions to part ways. The big difference between this situation and our traditional departures is that the leadership team feels good about the decision. Leaders have detached and know that they have done everything possible to assist the individual. The leaders can easily look in the mirror and know that they have provided an environment of positive regard and given every benefit to the employee to build awareness and take responsibility for their actions and outcomes. The leaders detach and do the right thing. They know that the employee needs a larger event in order to consider making the shift. The organization also realizes that enabling the employee to continue to reside in the victim mentality is not good for anyone. The leaders also know that the organization cannot say one thing and do another. If they have a person that is so negative, unhappy, and unwilling to make any changes, parting ways is the only option. It is intentional and follows a process that aligns with the accountability culture. You will know if the act of termination does not align with your values and new accountability culture if it doesn't feel good. Feeling some empathy for the person is normal, but it should not feel bad in any way for the organization. This is how we create sustainable change within organizations. This is how we shift our corporate culture to one of accountability based on love and compassion.

A Simple Case Study: The Absent Contributor

I use this case study when working with leaders practicing their coaching skills. Familiarize yourself with the characters and then pretend that you are Sandra, the outside coach, assisting Maggie in preparing for her discussion with her team. Frances is the director to whom Maggie reports. Jane is the absent contributor who is part of Maggie's team and Sandra who is going to assist Maggie in preparing to meet with her team.

Maggie has been running her department for over five years. She reports directly to Frances. Frances has been with the company for over 20 years and has been a director for over 8 years. Frances tends to see things black and white and likes to follow the rules. Some might say that she hides behind the rules and does not like working through complex people issues. She would rather make a decision and move on with little consultation. She is sometimes viewed by others as having a low emotional quotient.

Maggie has been dealing with an employee named Jane who has had significant attendance issues, missing more than the average in the department. This is a small department (10 employees) and the other employees have had to work harder to cover for Jane's absence. Jane does very specific work and there are not many people who can simply jump into the role. The department runs well and for the most part team members like working with each other but everyone is slowly getting tired of Jane always being away. Some team members are talking openly about how frustrated they are and a few have come to Maggie complaining. The department is in the middle of a very important project where Jane is a key player and it is beginning to impact the deliverables. The rest of the team feels that Jane has let them down.

Jane's absenteeism borders on discipline and formal follow up and some people believe that she is working the system to the best of her ability. Maggie is really tired of dealing with this and has been advising Frances along the way. Frances has no time for people who don't come to work and the conversations with Maggie about this are usually fairly negative. Frances has some strong judgments about Jane and her performance and attendance, even though Maggie has advised that when Jane is at work she is a reasonably strong performer. Frances' negative approach and black and white attitude has impacted how Maggie feels about Jane and has contributed to Maggie's negative feelings toward Jane.

Monday morning Jane arrives at work and requests a meeting with Maggie. She advises Maggie that she has been diagnosed with depression and is going to be off work for the next six weeks. She provides Maggie with a doctor's note and then leaves. Before leaving, Jane tells several of her colleagues about her extended absence. Maggie is sure that team members are going to be very angry as the project is at a critical stage.

Maggie informs Frances who says, "Look, I suspect that Jane doesn't really have depression and she is just working the system, however there isn't much we can do about it." Frances is kind of cynical and not a lot of help for Maggie. Maggie is frustrated and angry with Jane. Maggie appears to be taking it personally and feels that Jane has let the whole team down and especially her.

Sandra is a professional coach and is completely detached from the situation. Maggie has asked to meet with Sandra because she is really concerned about what to tell the employees that are left behind to pick up the extra work. Sandra agrees but notes that her role will be to coach Maggie.

Maggie knows that she will not be able to replace Jane on such short notice and so the team is going to have to work through it. Jane told many people in the office that she would be on an extended leave due to depression and therefore confidentiality is not as big an issue as it could have been. Maggie is sure that some staffs are going to want to process this situation out loud and many people are already starting to talk in the office about what Jane has done. Maggie expects team members to come to her tomorrow wanting to discuss the situation. Maggie doesn't know what to say and, in fact, has not processed her own feelings around this. She always felt that having a strong, reliable, and hardworking team was critical to success and she believes that Jane has let everyone down.

Take a few moments and consider what you would do. What questions would you ask Maggie in order for her to prepare for the following mornings meeting with her staff? What focus would you want to take?

What Do You Think Happened?

This is a difficult case. We often experience situations like this in the workplace. Now depending on the laws and rules in the country that you work, there may be some differences in how you would deal with this. In many countries there is a process for dealing with mental health concerns, and of course we want to be very sensitive to the unique requirements. When we use this case with our client groups we get a wide range of results and comments. Some of the groups will go to solving the immediate business issue of finishing the project on time. Others will spend a lot of time discussing whether they think Jane actually has depression or not. Other teams may discuss the need for training of staff in mental health sensitivity. Most teams will create questions to help assist Maggie in speaking with her team. Most of the teams become very creative, using all of the techniques discussed in previous sessions together.

This was a real case that came about in a leadership session many years ago. This particular class was a follow up to our coaching module. When Maggie, the manager, shared her difficult story in the session that afternoon, it was literally hours after Jane's departure. After asking her permission, we used this case as an example and had a group coaching session. As I asked Maggie questions she began to reflect. "Maggie, I want you to remember back to the last couple of times that Jane phoned in sick. Imagine those calls were happening right now. What did they *feel* like? How did Jane sound on the phone?" I wanted Maggie to *feel* the energy in those calls, to connect to her intuition and gut feel. I wanted her to connect to her heart center instead of going directly to the left brain. Maggie described Jane as not being herself and sensing that something was wrong. Based on Maggie's answers I asked her, "Do you think it is possible that Jane had been suffering from depression for some time and didn't even know it herself?" Maggie had described Jane as a great employee in the past with lots of energy and capability. Maggie took a deep breath and said, "Yes, I think it is very possible that Jane has been suffering from depression. Things have really changed for her." My next question was around her relationship with Frances. I asked, "Do you think you were being influenced by Frances' approach to the problem?" Of course, Maggie immediately realized that she had been negatively impacted by Frances' cold and direct approach to the problem. I then asked, "Do you think that you may be unintentionally influencing your team in feeling negatively frustrated by Jane's absence?" This was a big one for Maggie because she realized that she was doing to her employees exactly what Frances was doing to her. Remember, energy flows. Maggie was out of her personal alignment. I then asked Maggie, "Does it really matter whether Jane has depression or not and will we ever really know for sure?" Of course the answer was no. Then I asked another question that might seem sharp or prickly, but I wanted Maggie to have some further awareness of the power of human behavior and positive regard. I asked, "Maggie, if this was your son or daughter (meaning if Jane was your son or daughter) how would you want her employer and teammates to respond?"

The entire group of leaders in this class was all reflecting on this question. The next question that I asked the group of leaders was, "What do you think Maggie should do when she meets with her team tomorrow?" This is easy, Maggie could take her entire team on the same journey she had just been on, a journey of discovery and reflection that might allow them to see the situation differently, without Maggie telling them to. Maggie could ask the same questions, allow the team time to process and reflect, and then allow them to determine what to do with the extra work.

The greatest part about human nature is that people are basically good at heart and when we apply the rules of positive regard, we get positive regard in return. Maggie did exactly that and the team stepped up with no additional resources and finished the project on time and within budget. Frances was happy because she got what she wanted and Maggie built a collective energy within her team that was unstoppable. The other outcomes that needed to be addressed were that Jane was going to return to work. The question was, would she return to a group of angry, frustrated team members or a group of people who would welcome her back and be proud of their contributions in her absence? Would their independent and confident approach to the project make it easier for Jane to return?

Summary

The coaching conversation is so important. It is what truly changes the game for contributors at all levels. At its core, coaching is about creating new neural connections in the brain, through the process of exploration and discovery for both parties. It is about building a new realization within others and ourselves that can begin to change thought patterns, emotions, and, of course, behaviors.

When coaching is commenced after the leader has done all of their work and has followed the accountability model and its process, it can be, and often is, life changing for both parties. Unfortunately coaching is often taught to leaders around the world like a checklist. In many coaching courses the leader is taught the core competencies of being a good coach. Some of those might be staying open, listening with intensity, exploration for the purpose of discovery, great questioning, and so on. All of this is really important. However, when the leader has not built a very strong process for themselves first and foremost, the coaching can fall short, and end up being another program collecting dust on the shelf. Culture change requires a full and comprehensive understanding of human behavior and the new sciences, along with a committed approach by each leader to do the work of a new world leader.

CHAPTER 12

A Leader's Self-Care and Daily and Weekly Practices

As you can see, there is nothing easy about integrating the specific techniques and tools of the Accountability Model. It requires a significant shift on the part of the leader, both personally and professionally. The most successful leaders create daily practices that honor their intellectual, spiritual, physical, and emotional needs. They quickly understand that they are a complex being with unique needs that only they can take care of. This chapter is dedicated to exploring some new practices that will assist the leader in truly connecting to themselves in order to internalize the new tools.

There are many ways to create a smooth transition and each leader needs to consider, reflect, and try the practices that resonate with them. The primary goal of daily and weekly practices is to proactively reduce stress in the body and find new ways to quiet the mind and relax. A connection to one's breath is often a first step. This creates clarity, connection to oneself, and a real opportunity to build awareness. Good decision making requires good energy and a balanced state, especially in very busy and high stakes environments. Some of the suggestions I will reference are firmly backed by good research and are known to have a positive impact on a person's overall well-being. Other practices are simply things we have tried and seen great results. The hundreds of leaders we have worked with share what has worked and what has not. In the following sections, we share with you the things that have had visible and sustainable positive impact on leaders.

Nature

Why do most of us feel better when we are out in nature? What is this all about? Leaders often respond by saying, "There is a simple connection that occurs that makes us feel better." Leaders describe an instant ability to drop their shoulders and breathe more deeply. Some leaders are naturally drawn to nature, while others have to work at this one. Nature can be one of the most healing tools available to us. A simple commitment to have an intentional walk each evening with your dog or to go to the park each weekend can provide some immediate relief, especially for leaders who have not done this in a long time.

Many leaders come home from work, have a quick meal, and then get back to e-mail or other work for an hour or two. Decompression can be watching an hour of television with a beer and then they top the night off with a good dose of national news. We then wonder why we don't sleep well or why our minds are so active that falling asleep can be a challenge. The brain and body need a break. If you make a simple change in our routine like a nutritious meal and walk in nature followed by a really good book instead of the news you will be surprised how your sleep will suddenly become more effective. We have also been told that these simple changes have created better clarity for the leader the following day. My suspicion is that the better sleep is responsible. Sleep is so critical to clarity and mental and physical functioning.

Walking alone in nature and taking the time to notice the trees, grass, and sky is quite different than walking quickly in nature in order to get exercise while your mind is racing on what needs to be done tomorrow. The goal is to actually connect with nature. Notice the beauty and diversity of the scene. Any activity in the outside environment that is intentional, committed, and not strictly for exercise can have a positive impact. Beaches, sand, trees, and birds, all assist us in reconnecting to our innate humanness.

A Note on News

When we first begin working with leaders, we often discover that some leaders are news fanatics. They watch the news every day and often several times per day. The challenge for leaders who need and want to make the shift is that news is usually old energy, focused on the negativity in the world not all of the great things that are going on. The reason people sometimes have trouble sleeping after watching the news is that they have quietly and subtly changed their body chemistry. They have watched all of the negative things going on and have been affected by the pain and suffering. It is difficult not to be. As mentioned in previous chapters, we can experience an increase in the negative stress hormones before we realize it. It can put us into a state of being hyperalert, fight or flight, without us being consciously aware of it. I am not an advocate of being completely ignorant of what is happening around the world but I also don't believe that you need to watch large syndicated news broadcasts in order to be reasonably informed. The Internet allows us to get what we need without watching all of the other pieces that don't bring value. We can get the high level information we need without the intense negativity.

Some leaders we work with have made a conscious decision not to watch the news or follow any substantial news feeds. Many discovered it did not negatively impact their business decision making or overall connection to their working world. However, they did get to benefit from all of the positive impacts of not being exposed to the negativity. Again, this is your choice. If you are a news junkie, you might want to ask yourself what the value is of this activity and what the personal impact is to your energy. Remember that emotions are energy in motion so it does matter. If you feel a need to stay connected then limit the amount, source, and timing so that you are not exposing yourself right before sleeping.

Yoga, Tai Chi, Qi Gong

Our ability to find healthy ways to release energy, connect to our physical body, and learn to breathe again are all so important when we are making the shift to becoming a New World Leader. Our present society, although awakening, is not primarily focused on the importance of this type of connection. We have convinced people that physical exercise, like running and going to the gym to pump iron, is very important to our health, which of course is true in moderation. Stress hormones like cortisol can be released through exercise. However, it is important not to overburden our bodies with a sense that relentless pumping iron or running four marathons each year is a requirement.

Gentle, quiet exercise that is designed to connect the participant to their breath is also important. During times of stress most of us hold our breath and don't even realize it. At minimum, we are not aware of our breathing and the impacts it has on so many systems within our body, including brain function.

Eastern forms of exercise like yoga, tai chi, and qi gong are used extensively to reduce stress and connect the person to him or herself. This type of exercise is very intentional, slow, and precise. Some of these forms of exercise originated from specific religious practices. In today's context, they are offered throughout the world as simple ways to relax, connect to oneself, and breath.

I don't want to imply that running a marathon is bad or that going to the gym is not good. I am simply suggesting that we understand the energy and emotions that are at play when making these decisions. A wonderful balance of dynamic exercise combined with less dynamic exercise is important in finding balance. Connecting to the physical body each and every day is a very important practice. This can happen with any intentional and deliberate physical exercise.

Meditation

Many organizations are integrating meditation practices and training into their professional development initiatives. This is because they have been proven to be highly effective in reducing stress and creating better clarity. Meditation reduces heart rate and lowers blood pressure. It helps to reduce the stress hormones produced from overwork. There are numerous other benefits to this practice. I will provide several examples and encourage you to consider doing more research as these practices are known to be very instrumental in mind clarity and connection to personal alignment.

One of the most important results of meditation is our ability to slow down and clear the mind. Our incessant conversations with our room-mate or ego can be very detrimental to our overall health. As noted in an article published in the *Huffington Post* and written by Kristine Crane, there are eight key ways that meditation can improve your life (Crane 2014). Many of these are directly related to what the research tells us about great leadership. The benefits of meditation are described in the article as: reduces stress, improves concentration, encourages a healthy lifestyle, increases self-awareness, increases happiness, increases acceptance of what is, and slows aging. The research also identifies that meditation improves cardiovascular health and immune functioning. One of the other indications discovered through Dr. Richard Davidson's research with very experienced meditators is the link to improved neuroplasticity through meditation (Davidson and Lutz 2007). This means that our brains become more able to change with an active meditation practice. A regular meditation practice gives us an opportunity to slow the internal conversation and ultimately create more intentional dialogue that is positive.

In order to keep meditation simple and easy, begin by ignoring many of the rules you have read or heard about. You don't need special clothes, a special chair, special room, or fancy music. You simply need a quiet place where you will be uninterrupted. There are many different forms of meditation so stay open to the vast variety of mediation practices. One of the senior executives of a global IT company that I have worked with uses a form of dynamic meditation that was practiced by Osho for many years. Osho (Bhagwan Shree Rajneesh) was a famous mystic who wrote many books that are widely read today by those seeking balance and well-being. This senior executive openly attests to the benefits of reducing stress and connecting to their higher mind in a very intentional and constructive way. There are several Osho Meditation Centers around the world. One of the very informative online presences can be found at http://osho.com/meditate. Many of the Osho meditations create a loud, motion-filled mediation where the person is given an opportunity to release tons of stored up energy, frustration, and even anger. I have practiced several of Osho's meditations with great results, but I like a quiet reflective meditation where I practice to remove all of the dialogue in my head, where my mind can become quiet and peaceful. It is different for every person.

Another client made a very conscious decision to take on a meditation practice. It is important to note that practice is the correct word as it is not something that you perfect, it is a daily practice, like yoga. This client is very successful in spite of his busy lifestyle that rarely allows for any quiet reflective time. When he made the commitment, I was a little shocked and wondered how it would go. I was also very excited for him, as I knew just how much conversation he had going on with his roommate. Month, after month, after month, he practiced every day, and would report that he simply could not quiet his mind. When this gentleman makes up his mind, he does not give up so he stuck with it. Eight months later, he e-mailed me to say how he was finally getting it. He was transforming his life through meditation. He was experiencing a quiet and peaceful energy that he had never felt before. He said that he was able to keep that quiet energy through much of the day. His decision making was easier and more balanced and his results, both professionally and personally, were amazing.

The only recommendation I would provide for consideration when it comes to quiet meditation is to observe your breathing. You don't have to use special breathing or change your breathing in any way but our ability to focus on our breath by observing it is very helpful in being able to slow the chatter. In the early days of meditation, we often find that our minds will wander as we are not used to seeking stillness. Simply observe the conversation, don't judge it and then let it go. Remind yourself that this quiet time is for you.

A recent article, written by Silvia Damiano of *About My Brain*, shares valuable information on the impacts of meditation on leadership skills (Damiano 2017). In her interview with Dr. Fred Travis, director of the Center for Brain, Consciousness and Cognition at the Maharishi University of Management in Iowa states,

> From a leadership perspective, the results of consistent and effective meditation are profound. It can lead to better physical health and more efficient cognitive functioning—the high level of calm thinking that leaders need to consistently perform at their best.

Mindfulness

Mindfulness is the practice of getting quiet and becoming present in the moment. What better way to assist our practice of becoming the observer then learning to be present in the moment? So much of our time is spent thinking about things in the past or worrying about things in the future that have not happened yet. Our ability to truly be present is one of the most important leadership skills. How can we sense a room, feel the energy, and monitor the unspoken communication that is so impactful to our businesses if we do not know how to be present?

Mindfulness is so important in helping us learn to be present with our employees and those that are seeking our attention. I am not sure that we are a species designed to be busy all of the time, filling every moment with texts, e-mails, phone calls, and meetings. When we race from one thing to the other we learn to do things quickly with less attention. Research shows that attention is a critical skill to overall well-being and that learning to give 100 percent attention to our environment and interactions assist us in many ways. In Dr. Richard Davidson's video called "Well-Being is a Skill" he explains some of the research he has done in the area of attention and mindfulness (Wisdom 2.0 2015). Slowing our breathing, quieting the mind, and relaxing the body when we are not at work have a fabulous positive impact on our ability to be present at work.

Google has taken the practice of mindfulness to the next level by offering a customized course to assist leaders in going inward, creating meditation practices, and applying mindfulness at work. One of their senior engineers, Chade-Meng Tan, recently published a book called *Search Inside Yourself.*

> For the benefits of meditation to become widely accessible to humanity, it cannot just be the domain of bald people in funny robes living in mountains or small groups of New Age folks in San Francisco. It needs to align with the lives and interests of real people. (Tan 2012)

The book is all about their work in mindfulness and meditation and how they help all contributors to improve brain clarity, communication, and listening skills.

Journaling

Many people find that taking notes about their work, interactions, thoughts, and feelings assists them in processing situations and events. In many cases it allows the person to process how they feel and to reflect why they feel the way they do. The act of writing something out often makes it more real. There is something so cathartic about writing. Of course this does not work for all people and often men struggle more with journaling. When we work with men, we often talk about taking notes on how things went instead of journaling. Taking notes in a notebook seems to work better for some people.

I had one client who purchased a lovely journal. She told me that she didn't think she would ever be able to write anything in it. My guess was that deep down she was concerned that if she started writing she would never stop. I suspected through our coaching that she had lots of bottled up emotions that were now starting to impact her work life. Every time we met, she would state that the journal was with her in her purse along with a nice new pen. However, "I haven't written in it yet." At one meeting she said she even took it on a three-week vacation in hopes that she would get the urge but nothing happened. Committed to keeping it with her so that she could begin at any time, one day she simply started writing and as suspected, she just couldn't stop. Her ability to process her thoughts and feelings onto paper and to see what she had written was a process of building awareness and understanding. Most importantly, it is a process of letting go and feeling better. This is exactly what happened.

The Gratitude Jar

One of my favorite techniques is the practice of feeling and acknowledging gratitude for the things in our lives. So often we focus on the things we don't have which only creates negative emotions and we know what happens when that becomes prolonged. When we begin to have a daily gratitude practice, we begin to see the world in a very different light.

Writing in a journal each evening, the things you are grateful for, is helpful but one of my favorite tools is the gratitude jar. A client shared with me their daily practice and described a lovely jar that sits in their kitchen. Each day each member of the family takes a few moments to record something that they were grateful for that day. It goes into the jar. She stated it was a wonderful ritual she has with her children but both herself and her husband participate as well. The jar quickly fills up. On the off day where one of her children comes home with a worry or she or her husband have received bad news, they empty the gratitude jar and sit as a family reading each message. It can be a family event or an individual event but the goal is to remind ourselves of all the things we have to be grateful for. This practice can be very powerful as a leader who deals with difficulties often. The stress and worries of business can create a replaying of negative thoughts and negative energy. Practicing gratitude each and every day, either privately in your quiet moments or actively as a family, is very important to well-being and happiness.

Summary

Those that do research on the topics of happiness and well-being, such as Shawn Achor and Dr. Richard Davidson through the Center for Healthy Minds to name only two, have concluded that gratitude, acts of kindness, meditation, journaling, and mindfulness are important practices. They have also linked these practices to better learning, increased plasticity of the brain, and overall health.

We have had leaders who simply decided to breathe, and to notice their breathing, at specific times in the day. Even this simple practice has provided significant stress reduction and clarity. Some will set aside 10 minutes, 3 times a day, to close their office door, and practice slow intentional breathing where they sink into their chair and truly empty their minds. Many use this practice before all-important meetings. We have several highly extroverted Type A clients whose screen savers are the word *breathe* in large bold letters. This simple reminder is so helpful for them when dealing with daily challenges, coaching another person or when they feel overwhelmed.

Whatever you decide to do in support of your leadership transformation it is important to take action. Try different combinations of daily practices and see what resonates with you. Trust that there is something out there that can truly make a difference in your stress, brain clarity, and overall well-being. If we want our employees to make the shift, we must first make the shift ourselves. We cannot expect our employees to do something we are not willing to do ourselves. When we set the example and model the way, it is not long before our team members want to know what is going on and what you are doing in order to stay balanced, aligned, and happy even though some of your outer world may not have changed yet. This creates a totally new conversation.

CHAPTER 13

Putting It All Together

Leadership development that is life changing is at the core of creating the accountability culture. Gone are the days of the 10 Steps to Great Leadership, the Eight Laws of Successful Leaders or the 12 Attributes of Those at the Top. Instead, our focus is on creating a gentle balance between activating the intellect with new and exciting science, while exploring our emotional capacity, combined with a willingness to understand what it is to be truly human. I refer to this as the gentle balance between science and spirituality and our willingness to be open enough to explore who we really are.

The new sciences of neuroplasticity, quantum physics, and epigenetics help to enlighten us on the power of mind and emotions. The cutting edge research on the heart, intuition, and the magnetic energy field that surrounds us serves to expand our awareness of who we truly are and what we might be capable of. We are only beginning to understand the innate individual power we each hold within us.

When organizations make the courageous choice to shift their culture from old to new, they embark on a journey of incredible exploration. They begin to experience the power of each individual and, more importantly, the collective energy of a group of aligned people. This process is not easy and it doesn't happen overnight, but the rewards are so profound and exciting as organizations look for new and powerful ways to create sustainability and optimal performance.

These organizations are prepared to make the tough decisions when a person chooses to remain stuck in the old energy platform. The organization knows that regardless of great technical skills, if a leader or individual contributor is unwilling to step into their goo and learn to stretch, explore, engage in humility and grace, the organization will lose credibility if they allow these individuals to remain. However, they don't give up easily and they truly believe that every person has the capability to shift if given the right environment and honest encouragement.

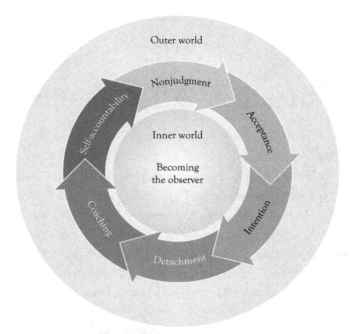

Figure 13.1 The accountability model

The Accountability Model as shown in Figure 13.1 is designed to provide a roadmap to access what we already innately know about ourselves. Deep down inside, we all have the ability to step back and own our own results, knowing that we create our experiences and outcomes through thoughts, feelings, emotions, and behaviors. No one else is responsible for how we feel or the results we get. That does not mean that bad things do not happen to nice people but what we decide to do with those experiences can be the difference between positive momentum with positive results or negative emotions with negative results. This does not mean that we should not process our true emotions in an honest way. The goal is to identify our emotions and ask the important questions about them. Our emotions tell us important things about ourselves. Pushing them down only creates issues in the future. Understanding our emotions and reflecting upon them is critical. It is like connecting the dots between heart and head, intellect and emotions. They both serve each other well and inform us in a balanced way.

No one likes to be judged. So why do we judge situations and people all the time with only a small portion of the information? We were taught and trained to do this whether it feels right or wrong. However, we now know that we can unlearn things and prune away neural connections that do not serve us. Start today to monitor your judgments and catch yourself. The more you observe yourself and your judgments, the earlier you will catch yourself and before you know it you will be open, observant, and neutral. This does not mean you won't have your own opinion, you just won't try to convince people they need to agree with you and you will not have the negative emotions that occur when disagreements happen because you won't be boulder pushing. Our ability to simply accept things and people as they are allows us to also stay more balanced. Acceptance does not mean agreement but simply that you are not emotional about someone else's decisions or actions. You observe them and accept them for what they appear to be.

When dealing with events, people, and situations, we need to dig deep regarding our true intention, especially when we are in a leadership role. We need to guide and facilitate outcomes. If our intentions when we enter conversations, are all about the organization, team, and you the leader, we set ourselves up for the stress response in the other person. Why do we make someone else's behavior about us? Why do we internalize someone else's stuff and allow it to impact us? Keep it separate. Then stay open, curious, and willing to explore for the sake of helping yourself to better understand, and for the other person to build awareness. Your intentions can be positive and engaging. Seeking feedback from the other person, instead of giving feedback, builds trust and does not ignite the stress hormones, which can result in the defensive behavior we commonly experience when having difficult conversations. The other person will feel your openness and willingness. We know that everything is energy including our emotions. They are simply energy in motion and, as a result, we must monitor our emotions when dealing with business issues.

If we are attached to a specific outcome that involves another person, we must be careful to ask ourselves how our attachments (emotions) will serve the conversation. When the leader stays attached, they continue to own the responsibility, and this is the energy they put out. The leader keeps the issues squarely on their side of the table. When the leader can detach from the outcome, knowing that it is not theirs, they are more likely to be able to place the responsibility, through great coaching, squarely on the other side of the table where it belongs. Whether the other person takes the responsibility is up to them and them alone. We always have our old mechanistic tools to go back to if we have to, but this should only be a last resort. Detaching is one of the hardest skills a leader can learn but is truly the most impactful. A sense of relief ensues almost automatically as we stop owning everyone else's stuff. We begin to relax and, most importantly, we can care deeply without being attached to the outcome.

It is time for all leaders to go inside and search for the truth that lies within each of us. We intuitively know that love and compassion, trust and integrity are all part of who we once were and that these attributes are still within us. We are more likely to create amazing long-term results in business when these skills are brought back up to the surface, honored and celebrated. Our old energy techniques are dying and intuitively we know that they do not work, especially in today's world. If we want happy, balanced, and highly effective employees we must be happy, balanced, and highly effective leaders. We must go back to our roots and explore our natural abilities to create environments of trust, caring, and compassionate cultures that connect to a compelling purpose.

In these new energy cultures all contributors are comfortable enough to be honest before kind while doing the hard work of monitoring intention. They also take full and honest responsibility for the outcomes they get. A true accountability culture is not exposed to the encroachment of the victim mentality. It is impossible for it to take hold.

In these new energy organizations, the leaders know that personal self-care is critical and they do not apologize for seeking and finding balance. They understand and are supported to have appropriate breaks during work hours, to apply mindfulness, and to balance the energy and emotions through meditation, gratitude, and acts of kindness. These leaders also know that not everyone will want to come along for the ride and that it is absolutely OK to know when a team member has decided it is too hard and does not want to make the shift. The difference between can't and won't is in play and leaders have no guilt or hard feelings when they have to part ways with an employee because they can solidly look in the mirror and know that they did everything they could to assist in building awareness.

After a hundred years of mechanistic carrot-and-stick management, it is time to shift our energy to one of positivity and compassion, to create environments where caring and open dialogue transforms and enlightens all of our thinking around business results, optimal performance, and accountability. Our employees are human beings and therefore innately want to be accountable for their emotions, behaviors, actions, and results. Our job is to simply create the environment where this can flourish.

In the future, improving corporate results will not be about undercutting your competitors, working harder and faster than others, or having a better marketing campaign. It will be about how to create a positive culture, utilizing positive psychology and neuroscience and encouraging everyone to tap into what it is to truly be human. It will include recognizing all contributors' innate abilities to monitor what they think about, take responsibility for how they feel and their resulting outcomes. Personal accountability will be at the focus of performance but instead of it having a negative energy or connotation, it will have a truly positive one. It will be where employees take their power back in a constructive and safe way that creates unstoppable results. This is the new accountability culture.

References

Achor, S. 2010. *The Happiness Advantage: The Seven Principles of Positive Psychology That Fuel Success and Performance at Work*, 44. New York, NY: Crown Business.

Albert, S., B.E. Ashforth, and J.E. Dutton. 2000. "Organizational Identity and Identification: Charting New Waters and Building New Bridges." *Academy of Management Review* 25, no. 1, pp. 13–17.

Arnsten, A.F.T. 2009. "Stress Signaling Pathways that Impair Prefrontal Cortex Structure and Function," *Nature Reviews Neuroscience* 10, no. 6, pp. 410–22.

Ashforth, B.E., and A.M. Saks. 2000. "Personal Control in Organizations: A Longitudinal Investigation with Newcomers," *Human Relations* 53, no. 3, pp. 311–39.

Bandura, A. 1986. *Social Foundations of Thought and Action: A Social Cognitive Theory.* Upper Saddle River, NJ: Prentice-Hall.

Bandura, A. 2001. "Social Cognitive Theory: An Agentic Perspective." *Annual Review of Psychology* 52, no. 1, pp. 1–26.

Baumeister, R.F., and M.R. Leary. 1995. "The Need to Belong: Desire for Interpersonal Attachments as a Fundamental Human Motivation," *Psychological Bulletin* 117, no. 3, pp. 497–529.

Caproni, P.J. 2012. *Management Skills for Everyday Life,* 3rd ed. Upper Saddle River, NJ: Prentice-Hall.

Center for Healthy Minds-University of Wisconsin-Madison. 2017. "Our Founder." https://centerhealthyminds.org/about/founder-richard-davidson (accessed July 17, 2017).

Change Innovators Inc. 2017. "New World Leadership™ Series." https://changeinnovators.com/leadership (accessed July 11, 2017).

ChartHouse Learning. 2001. *It's So Simple.* DVD.

Chouinard, Y. 2006. *Let My People Go Surfing: The Education of a Reluctant Businessman.* Toronto: Penguin Books.

Cook, J., and T. Wall. 1980. "New Work Attitude Measures of Trust, Organizational Commitment and Personal Need Non-fulfillment." *Journal of Occupational Psychology* 53, no. 1, pp. 39–52.

Crane, K. 2014. "8 Ways Meditation Can Improve Your Life." *HuffPost: Healthy Living* (blog), September 19. https://huffingtonpost.com/2014/09/19/meditation-benefits_n_5842870.html

Crane, T.G. 2012. *The Heart of Coaching.* San Diego: FTA Press.

Csikszentmihalyi, M. 1990. *Flow: The Psychology of Optimal Experience.* New York, NY: Harper & Row.

Damiano, S. 2017. "Why Meditation Is An Essential Tool In Our Leadership Performance." *About My Brain* (blog), August 29. http://blog.aboutmybrain.com/why-meditation-is-an-essential-tool-in-our-leadership-performance

Dar-Nimrod, I., and S.J. Heine. 2006. "Exposure to Scientific Theories Affects Women's Math Performance." *Science* 314, no. 5798, p. 435.

Davidson, R.J., and A. Lutz. September 2007. "Buddha's Brain: Neuroplasticity and Meditation." *IEEE Signal Processing Magazine* 25, no. 1, pp. 172–74.

Dominion Bank Rules, unknown newspaper source.

Edelman. 2012. "Executive Summary: 2012 Edelman goodpurpose® Study." http://scribd.com/doc/90411623/Executive-Summary-2012-Edelman-goodpurpose-Study (accessed July 14, 2017).

Feldman, M.S., and A. Rafaeli. 2002. "Organizational Routines as Sources of Connections and Understandings." *Journal of Management Studies* 39, no. 3, pp. 309–31.

Frankl, V.E. 1959. *Man's Search for Meaning.* New York, NY: Simon and Schuster.

HeartMath Institute. 2016. "Science of the Heart: Exploring the Role of the Heart in Human Performance." https://heartmath.org/research/science-of-the-heart/ (accessed July 11, 2017).

Kelvin, P. 1977. "Predictability, Power and Vulnerability in Interpersonal Attractions." In *Theory and Practice in Interpersonal Attractions*, ed. D. Steven. 355–78. London: Academic Press.

Krause, N., and B.A. Shaw. 2000. "Role-Specific Feelings of Control and Mortality." *Psychology and Aging* 15, no. 4, pp. 617–26.

Lao-tzu., and S. Mitchell. 1988. *Tao te ching: A New English Version*, chap. 33. New York, NY: Harper & Row.

Mayburov, S. 2012. "Photonic Communications and Information Encoding in Biological Systems." *arXiv*. Last modified May 2012. https://arxiv.org/abs/1205.4134

McCraty, R., M. Atkinson, and R.T. Bradley. 2004. "Electrophysiological Evidence of Intuition: Part 1. The Surprising Role of the Heart." *Journal of Alternative and Complementary Medicine* 10, no. 1, 133–43. https://heartmath.org/research/research-library/intuition/electrophysiological-evidence-of-intuition-part-1/

McCraty, R., M. Atkinson, D. Tomasino, and W.A. Tiller. 1998. "The Electricity of Touch: Detection and Measurement of Cardiac Energy Exchange Between People." In *Brain and Values: Is a Biological Science of Values Possible,* ed. K.H. Pribram. 359–79. Mahway, NJ: Lawrence Erlbaum Associates, Publishers. https://heartmath.org/research/research-library/energetics/electricity-of-touch/electricity-of-touch-02/

McLeod, S. 2016. "Maslow's Hierarchy of Needs." Last modified September 16. https://simplypsychology.org/maslow.html

Mehrabian, A. 1971. *Silent Messages*, 42–3. Belmont, CA: Wadsworth.

Merriam Webster, *s.v.* "energy." https://merriam-webster.com/dictionary/energy (accessed July 17, 2017).

Murphy Paul, A. 2011. "The Science of Intuition: An Eye-Opening Guide to Your Sixth Sense." *O Magazine*, July 14. http://oprah.com/spirit/Scientific-Facts-About-Intuition-Developing-Intuition (accessed July 17, 2017).

National Geographic. February 2016a. "The Science of a Happy Mind, Part 1." Filmed YouTube video, 14:18. Posted March 2016. https://youtube.com/watch?v=ELLeIMFIWy0

National Geographic. February 2016b. "The Science of a Happy Mind, Part 2." Filmed YouTube video, 13:55. Posted March 2016. https://youtube.com/watch?v= tKxD4G--amw

NeuroLeadership Institute. 2017. "NeuroLeadership Institute." https://neuroleadership.com (accessed July 17, 2017).

O'Reilly, C., and J. Chatman. 1994. "Working Smarter and Harder: A Longitudinal Study of Managerial Success," *Administrative Science Quarterly* 39, no. 4, pp. 603–28.

Patagonia. 2017. "Environmental & Social Responsibility." http://patagonia.ca/environmentalism.html (accessed July 14, 2017).

Paunonen, S.V., and R.Y. Hong. 2010. "Self-Efficacy and the Prediction of Domain-Specific Cognitive Abilities." *Journal of Personality* 78, no. 1, pp. 339–60.

Pink, D.H. 2009. *Drive: The Surprising Truth About What Motivates Us*, 57. New York, NY: Riverhead Books.

Shoshany, B. 2014. "What are Messenger Particles in QED?" https://quora.com/What-are-messenger-particles-in-QED (accessed September 7, 2017).

Singer, M. 2015. *The Surrender Experiment*. New York, NY: Crown Publishing Group.

Tan, C.-M. 2012. *Search Inside Yourself: The Unexpected Path To Achieving Success, Happiness (And World Peace)*. New York, NY: HarperOne.

The Ideal Changes. 2015. "Intuition The Power of the Heart Heartmath." YouTube video, 3:04. Posted July 8, 2015. https://youtube.com/watch?v=9q0UEH8fRzc

Wartzman, R. 2015. "What Unilever shares with Google and Apple," *Fortune*, January 7. http://fortune.com/2015/01/07/what-unilever-shares-with-google-and-apple/

Wisdom 2.0. 2015. "Well being is a Skill: Richard Davidson." YouTube video, 25:27. Posted March 30, 2015. https://youtube.com/watch?v=EPGJU7W0

Index

OTHER TITLES IN THE HUMAN RESOURCE MANAGEMENT AND ORGANIZATIONAL BEHAVIOR COLLECTION

- *Slow Down to Speed Up: Lead, Succeed, and Thrive in a 24/7 World* by Liz Bywater
- *Agile Human Resources: Creating a Sustainable Future for the HR Profession* by Kelly Swingler
- *Infectious Innovation: Secrets of Transforming Employee Ideas Into Dramatic Revenue Growth* by James Allan
- *21st Century Skills for Non-Profit Managers: A Practical Guide on Leadership and Management* by Don Macdonald and Charles Oham
- *Conflict First Aid: How to Stop Personality Clashes and Disputes from Damaging You or Your Organization* by Nancy Radford
- *How to Manage Your Career: The Power of Mindset in Fostering Success* by Kelly Swingler
- *Deconstructing Management Maxims, Volume I: A Critical Examination of Conventional Business Wisdom* by Kevin Wayne
- *Deconstructing Management Maxims, Volume II: A Critical Examination of Conventional Business Wisdom* by Kevin Wayne
- *The Real Me: Find and Express Your Authentic Self* by Mark Eyre
- *Across the Spectrum: What Color Are You?* by Stephen Elkins-Jarrett
- *The Human Resource Professional's Guide to Change Management: Practical Tools and Techniques to Enact Meaningful and Lasting Organizational Change* by Melanie J. Peacock
- *Tough Calls: How to Move Beyond Indecision and Good Intentions* by Linda D. Henman
- *The 360 Degree CEO: Generating Profits While Leading and Living with Passion and Principles* by Lorraine A. Moore

Announcing the Business Expert Press Digital Library

Concise e-books business students need for classroom and research

This book can also be purchased in an e-book collection by your library as

- a one-time purchase,
- that is owned forever,
- allows for simultaneous readers,
- has no restrictions on printing, and
- can be downloaded as PDFs from within the library community.

Our digital library collections are a great solution to beat the rising cost of textbooks. E-books can be loaded into their course management systems or onto students' e-book readers.
The **Business Expert Press** digital libraries are very affordable, with no obligation to buy in future years. For more information, please visit **www.businessexpertpress.com/librarians**. To set up a trial in the United States, please email **sales@businessexpertpress.com**.

Printed in the USA
CPSIA information can be obtained
at www.ICGtesting.com
JSHW011215090224
56986JS00003B/10

9 781948 198783